Praise for

not impossible

"A unique and inspiring journal of brave abandon. Mick's journey, along the thin border between naivete and genius, becomes a cautionary tale about caution itself—and how to learn to abandon it. It is the story of a free, open, maker world where the most uncommon ideas become common sense."

—Nicholas Negroponte, professor and co-founder of MIT Media Lab, founder of One Laptop per Child, author of *Being Digital*

"This is the template for a new science of consciousness. Mick Ebeling sees impossible just as a word for something not yet done. Read his book. Think like him. Then do the impossible."

—Deepak Chopra

"Mick Ebeling's been a friend of mine for a long time but, after reading *Not Impossible*, he's become one of my heroes."

—Matt Fraction

"This is a fantastic read if you want to change the world, change the system, or just change yourself. A perfect embodiment of the idea that 'the true revolutionary is guided by great feelings of love.'"

—Shepard Fairey

"*Not Impossible* is a masterful achievement: a road map to changing your life by changing the lives of others. The inspirational tales in this book show how to toss off old ways of thinking and look at the world from a new perspective. Mick has found a way to do just that."

—Jillian Michaels

not impossible

The Art and Joy of Doing
What Couldn't Be Done

MICK EBELING

ATRIA PAPERBACK

New York   London   Toronto   Sydney   New Delhi

ATRIA PAPERBACK
An Imprint of Simon & Schuster, Inc.
1230 Avenue of the Americas
New York, NY 10020

Copyright © 2015 by Leslie "Mick" Ebeling

First Atria Paperback edition February 2017

ATRIA PAPERBACK and colophon are trademarks of Simon & Schuster, Inc.

For information about special discounts for bulk purchases, please contact Simon & Schuster Special Sales at 1-866-506-1949 or business@simonandschuster.com.

The Simon & Schuster Speakers Bureau can bring authors to your live event. For more information or to book an event contact the Simon & Schuster Speakers Bureau at 1-866-248-3049 or visit our website at www.simonspeakers.com.

Design by Kyoko Watanabe

Manufactured in the United States of America

10 9 8 7 6 5 4 3 2 1

Library of Congress Cataloging-in-Publication Data

Ebeling, Mick.
Not impossible : the art and joy of doing what couldn't be done
    pages cm
Includes index.
    1. Ebeling, Mick. 2. Self-help devices for people with disabilities—United States.
    3. Inventions—United States. 4. Rehabilitation technology—United States.
    5. Biomedical engineering—United States. 6. Humanitarianism—United States.
    7. Businessmen—United States.   I. Title.
HV1569.5.E24 0215
681'.761092—dc23
[B]
                        2014029469

ISBN 978-1-4767-8280-5
ISBN 978-1-4767-8282-9 (pbk)
ISBN 978-1-4767-8283-6 (ebook)

Contents

Contents

To Dad, Mom, and Pamps
You made me possible

To Caskey, Angus, Bo, and Trace
You make me possible

Whether you think you can, or think you can't,
you're right.

—Henry Ford

not impossible

not impossible

CHAPTER 1

The New Old-Fashioned Way: Do It Yourself

It's been three days since the police let us go, but I'm still feeling pretty shaken up about it.

It's hard not to get paranoid when you've been arrested for taking a picture of a wheelbarrow.

Here in Juba, the old capital city of the relatively new country of South Sudan, this is supposed to be the dry season, but it's been raining every day. Juba is relatively developed compared with a lot of other cities and towns in this country, but most of the roads near our hotel are still unpaved, so I've gotten a great firsthand lesson in mud. There are two kinds of mud here: the normal brown mud that you're used to and a strange black slippery mud that feels sort of like molasses under your feet. It's almost impossible to walk on. Everywhere you look, someone has fallen and gotten covered in mud. No one seems too upset about it; they pick themselves up, don't stop to wipe themselves off, and they continue on their way.

In fact, every time someone falls in the mud here, people laugh. It's kind of disconcerting—your first reaction is, man, how rude, but then you realize that it makes its own kind of perfect sense.

You fall, you laugh.

Because you're not dead.

Such is life in a war zone. At least, that's how it feels to me, having spent a few days here among people who have faced unimaginable horrors. After what they've been through, I guess they have greater concerns than whether they happen to have mud on their clothes.

The rain doesn't seem to want to stop, and my biggest concern is that if it doesn't stop, the authorities may not let us take off from here. They're telling me the runways are too wet, and our plane is too heavy, and we won't be able to land in Yida, the site of a 70,000-person refugee camp near the Sudan border. And if I don't get out of here and get to Yida soon, I may go stark-staring crazy. Everything my team and I have been working on for months has led up to this: the trip to Yida.

So we are, quite literally, stuck in the mud.

Sitting here in limbo has given me some time to reflect on what we've been referring to as "this insane thing we're doing"—it'd be way too overblown to call it our mission, and we're way too disorganized to call it a plan. But we have a distinct goal ahead of us. Just a few months ago, I had the idea of coming to Africa when I first heard about Daniel, a boy whose arms were blown off in the war. About the same time, I had first heard about the possibility of creating new prosthetic arms, not through normal medical channels, but in a very do-it-yourself crazy hacker way—my way, in short—with an off-the-shelf 3-D printer.

And that's when the idea first occurred to me that I could make those arms for Daniel.

And I decided to try to do it.

While we've been waiting here in Juba to leave for the camp where Daniel is staying, I've gotten to meet a lot of people, and while there's a normality to their lives—no matter where you go, people do what they do, they get up and they go about their business and they eat and visit and try not to fall in the mud—there's a jitteriness to it all, too. The sense that violence and hostilities are never far beneath the surface either in the contested areas of Sudan or here in South Sudan, and that they are getting ready to explode again. That creates a real tension in the air. You can almost taste it.

These people have seen bombs rain down from the sky. They've seen their children's arms blown off right in front of them, their wives and husbands and children and babies and grandmothers killed, for no apparent reason. Being in their presence, you can feel the sense of impending disaster, like smelling rain in the air just before a storm.

Someone told me yesterday that every single person in this city has an AK-47 in their home. Probably an exaggeration, but still a pretty frightening thought.

We were taking some background photos the other day to document this insane thing we're doing and to pass the time before we leave to make the arms. As we were shooting the pictures, some children came running up to us, saying, in various languages, which our translators helped us keep track of, "Photo! Photo! Take my photo!"

Just when we were taking some photos of a nearby hut—a small structure with a blue wheelbarrow in front of it—a man who appeared to be a soldier, in a starched tan shirt and overly large aviator sunglasses, said something about the photos. But from his tone it was most certainly not "Take my photo!" The next thing I knew, we were all being hauled down to the police to explain what we were doing there.

Suddenly, I realized how very little I knew about South Sudan and how to accomplish what we were planning to accomplish.

I am not a medical person by trade. Nor am I a fabricator or a 3-D printing expert; nor do I know much about Africa, bombs, the SPLA—the Sudan People's Liberation Army—or just about anything we're doing, for that matter.

I'm a producer. I work on films and TV shows, I make commercials and trailers, I create videos for clients of all stripes. I've done the credit sequences for some big movies and the graphics for some others. I've started a few businesses, sat on some boards, launched some nonprofits.

So after the police decided not to detain us, and we were left to cool our heels in the rain and the mud in Juba, waiting for our chance to get up to the refugee camp in Yida, there was one question hanging in the air.

How the hell did I get here?

◆

I had tried to ignore that question on the initial flight over to Johannesburg from Los Angeles. That flight had been delayed a day because my dog Georgia, our beautiful brown boxer, my faithful friend for sixteen years, was dying, and it didn't feel right to leave without saying good-bye. We struggled all day about what to do—should we euthanize her before I left? It felt wrong. It felt like I was rushing it. So I delayed my flight the next day, and by the evening it was clear that she was waning, so we scheduled the doctor to come to our house at nine o'clock that night, and we all said our good-byes to her, my wife Caskey and our three boys and I.

The doctor was late; he showed up at the house at 9:37 p.m., precisely three minutes after Georgia miraculously popped up like a jack-in-the-box and started walking around the house, eating her food, and drinking her water. So when the doctor showed up and she started barking at him like crazy—and she's not the kind of dog who usually barks at visitors—he said, "Um, I'm not euthanizing her today. She's just not ready to go yet."

We took that as a very good sign, good karma for the trip. But on the flight over, as I caught up on my reading—books like *They Poured Fire on Us from the Sky*, a harrowing account of three of the Lost Boys of Sudan—I started coming to terms with where I was actually going. In Sudan, warring tribes and armies kill indiscriminately, rape indiscriminately, torture women and children and grown men. Journalists are as unwelcome as the ever-present mosquitoes, only easier to get rid of. I imagined my last words on this earth being "I am not a journalist!" and I realized how little I was really prepared for the journey ahead of me.

But I had also spent the last two years in the company of extraordinary gentlemen and women—crazy lunatic gentlemen and women, to be precise. I was taking this trip on behalf of Not Impossible Labs, a company I'd created to try to solve medical problems that seemed to be unsolvable, and beyond that, to solve them in a very Do-It-Yourself kind of way. To get around the big medical companies, the big insurance companies, the big everything. To just get our hands dirty and take the backs off things, figure out how they work, and jerry-rig something new that could do the job just as well and then give it away for free.

The people who populated our lives now, the people who were helping me along this wild and crazy path, defined themselves as hackers and "makers"—which is how I defined myself now, too.

That's what this book is about. It's about Doing It Yourself and redefining what it means to Do It Yourself.

A light rain was falling outside the plane, and I found myself hypnotized by the blinking red light on the wing, as I thought about the concept of Do It Yourself. It's as old as the loom and as new as the 3-D printer. Some say DIY is actually changing the way the American economy itself works. I'm not sure about that, but it sure is changing the way I work. And changing the way we think.

I am an executive producer by trade, and I could have executive-produced this trip—meaning, I could have secured the funding, hired the personnel, arranged the travel, laid out the itinerary, imbued the team with the goals of the mission, been the cheerleader and the scold and the teacher and the planner and all the other things that an executive producer does. And then I could have sent everybody on their way with my sincere best wishes.

But at some point, I guess, the do-it-yourself concept actually involves doing it yourself. So instead of executive-producing this trip, I found myself on this plane, in the rain, in the dark, doing something far different than anything I'd ever done before.

In a few hours, I would be landing in Johannesburg. I'd spend a week, at best, learning how to make a mechanical hand with a 3-D printer and some parts we'd picked up at a hardware store—using techniques that others have taken months to perfect. To distract myself, I turned my attention to the in-flight movie *The Blind Side*, in which Sandra Bullock adopts a poor kid who happens to be a great football player. Toward the end of the film, I found myself crying, tears slowly dripping down my cheeks, mimicking the rain that was streaking the airplane windows. In-flight movies always seem to make me cry; something to do with the jetlag and the strange air and the helpless feeling of being propelled at 600 miles an hour in a big metal Tylenol capsule, and the blind faith inherent in that activity.

But if I'm being honest, I was probably crying for another reason.

As the movie ended, I got up to walk around the cabin a bit before we touched down. The sun started coming up on the left side of the plane. A new day was beginning, in more ways than one, for me. Behind me, back in LA, my boys were going to get ready for their first Halloween without me and, quite possibly, our first Thanksgiving apart as well. Ahead of me—well, I had no idea of what was ahead of me.

But in this transition moment—between my past and my future, really—I found myself contemplating the answer to that overwhelming question: What had brought me to this place, this place where I was taking a leap of faith into the unknown? Where I believe that there are ways to defy the odds and the naysayers and your own insecurities and accomplish what everybody tells you is impossible. How had I gotten to this place where that was going to be put to the ultimate test?

Could I really make the impossible possible?

And could I do it in a way that's translatable—that I could share with others, so they could make the impossible possible as well?

I didn't know the answer to that.

But I did know one thing.

I was about to, quite literally, stake my life on it.

CHAPTER 2

Yes Is So Much More Fun

I should make one thing clear right away.

I did not set out in life to be the guy who goes to the Sudan with a 3-D printer, trying to create new arms for a kid who had his blown off in the war. I did not set out in life to create a foundation and a company that invites people to write in about their unsolvable medical problems, or to put together teams of hackers, artists, poets, philosophers, and crazies of all stripes to see if they could solve them.

I did not set out to discover the power of Yes or the stunning energy that comes from surrendering yourself to the Not Impossible way of life. I did not set out to discover what that surrendering can do for your business, or what it can do for your soul, although in the years that followed, the power of Yes became all-consuming, the guiding light that lit my days and warmed my nights and showed me where to plant my feet if I wanted to stand up straight.

I did not set out to do any of those things.

I set out to go surfing.

It was coming on New Year's Eve, at the turn of the millennium (or the turn of the calendar to 2000, anyway; the purists say that the millennium didn't really start until 2001, but I have very little need in my life or my business for purists). My wife, Caskey, and I decided to celebrate the momentous day in Costa Rica. A few days later, we broke off for a little mini-vacation-in-a-vacation at a B and B in Mal Pais, a tiny village on the Pacific side of the country.

We couldn't have gotten more out of the way, which is what we wanted. We were a thousand miles from the crowded break that I surf back home, and as we drove our four-wheeler down a dirt road to the beach, nearly putting our wheels in a ditch to avoid the kids coming back from the beach on motorcycles, one hand on the handlebars and a surfboard under the other, their day already done as ours was just beginning, from the look and feel of it it might as well have been a million miles away.

When the waves are pumping, the break off Mal Pais is a challenging place to surf, which is what I was looking for. Some breaks are easy to read, and some breaks are a challenge. Ever since I was a kid, it was the challenge that turned me on: If there wasn't a little bit of danger to what I was doing, a little sense of jumping without a net, I didn't see the point.

You have to be a little like that in business, I think. If you're always worrying about what-if-I-fail, you're never going to give yourself much of a chance to succeed. And there's nothing quite like surfing in cross-currents and sudden swells to remind you to live only in the moment and think only of success: The moment you start to doubt yourself, you're never gonna make the drop.

Caskey was reading on the beach and I was paddling out and getting ready to catch a wave, feeling pretty good. There are moments out there on the surf, when the sun is glinting off the water in a thousand shimmering diamonds of light, when the wind is offshore and the spray of the breaking waves seems to hold the droplets of water in the air for just an extra moment before letting them settle back into the ocean, when this is the only place you can imagine ever wanting to be, and all is right with the world.

And then some big hairy guy paddles up and yells, "Hey! Yo! How you doing?" and screws up the whole thing.

I mean, no kidding, you're surfing by yourself in a desolate little town, you've traveled a thousand miles from your home break, and all you want is to have the break to yourself. Not to share it with some loud dude with bright orange ear plugs who's crowding your wide-open space.

When I look back on it now, though, there's something karmic in that moment. There I was, trying to put a wall all around my world, a high round wall with me at the center of it, and that wall was knocked down. When I look back on it now, there's no better symbol of everything that I was about to learn, everything that was about to happen to me.

But that's now. That wasn't then. Then, all I could think was: Shut up. Go away. Let me return to my perfect moment.

That was not to be.

"Ubi! Ubi!" the guy yelled at me. At first, I didn't think he was speaking English. I speak Spanish pretty well but couldn't figure out what he was trying to tell me.

"Ubi! You?" he yelled over the crash of the waves. Do I . . . ubi? I wasn't sure what to say.

"Lo siento, amigo, no entiendo," I tried. Sorry, pal, I don't understand.

"I said I'm Ubi," he yelled back. "Who are you?"

Oh.

We jabbered away for a while, floating along on our boards, and after a few minutes, I realized that Ubi was a pretty nice guy. Loud, mind you, since he had the ear plugs in, but a really nice guy, in fact. The more we talked, the lousier I felt about skewering him in my mind for a jerk who'd stolen my personal surf spot. I mean, here I was, some tourist who'd gotten here five minutes before he had, and I'm acting like I own the beach, so who's the jerk? Fortunately, Ubi was such a jovial and outgoing guy, any tension that I might have projected washed over him like the next wave headed for shore. We surfed together for a couple of hours, and on one of the passes I noticed that he seemed to have come with someone, a woman, and she had struck up a conversation with Caskey under the shade of a big, wild, overgrown palm tree.

When we finally padded into the shore, he introduced her as his girlfriend. She was stunning: statuesque and stately, with perfect hair and perfect skin and perfect everything else. And what crossed my mind was what crosses the mind of any man who meets a supermodel-hot woman with a not-so-perfect looking guy: What the hell is she doing with him?

As the day passed on into evening, and we hung out and met for drinks later on, I figured it out. Ubi was one of the most fun, effervescent guys you'd ever want to meet. He was even bigger than he seemed in the water—six-foot-five, somewhere north of 270 pounds—but his personality was twice that size.

We had lunch with them, and dinner, and the next day at breakfast we walked into the dining room, and he was frantically waving his arms for us to join him. By this point I was feeling that fun's fun, but a romantic getaway's a romantic getaway, and it seemed like Caskey and I hadn't spent five minutes alone together since we'd met Ubi and his girlfriend, so I begged off, and I swear, his face dropped so fast I thought his chin was going to crash into the cornflakes. It wasn't until later, when I met up with him for a drink in New York, that I got the full story. When I asked him how his girlfriend was, he laughed hard and loud, then explained: He was sorry he'd been so emotionally clingy down in Costa Rica, but as beautiful as that woman was, she was driving him batshit crazy on vacation, and they'd broken up right after that.

Somehow, having had that experience together made us into fast friends—like we'd known each other for years—although with a guy like Ubi, I'm guessing that's not hard. Just a nice guy, loud as the engine on my '64 Wildcat and twice as powerful when it comes to driving a party forward. In the months and years that followed, he was around a lot, and we developed a phrase: Want to have a party? Just add Ubi.

◆

Over the course of the next seven years, a lot of things changed in our lives—Caskey and I moved, we had children, we started businesses, we bought a house. But a few things stayed constant. One was date night; the more complicated our lives became, the more important it was to have a ritual that reminded us that there was something beyond work by day and diapers and feedings by night. Don't get me wrong—I love my three boys with a passion that surpasses words or understanding—but at least once in a while you need to go have dinner and see a movie alone with an actual grown-up who you're actually married to and has seen you naked and still loves you.

Another thing that stayed constant in our lives was Ubi. Caskey and I had moved into a nice new house in Venice Beach. We installed an electronic combination lock on the front gate because it wasn't the best of neighborhoods at the time, but most of our friends knew the combination from house-sitting or babysitting or just coming by at some point, and a few of them used the knowledge to just walk in unannounced when they felt like it. And on this particular night, as we were primping for our date night, that was Ubi.

"YO! YO!! WHAT'S GOING ON!" he boomed, more a statement than a question. He had another friend in tow, a guy named Rojelio, who was as quiet as Ubi was loud.

"Hey, man," I said. "How you doing? We're getting ready to go have dinner and see a movie at the—"

"No, you're not!" Ubi interrupted. "You're coming with us!"

It takes about five seconds for disappointment to turn into curiosity, less when you know you're surrendering to the inevitable. Somehow I knew that no matter what I said, we were going to wind up bending to the force of Ubi's will. He was so up and excited—I mean, even for him, this seemed like a high moment—that I didn't even bother to argue. I looked over at Caskey, and by the smile on her face, I could tell she was thinking the same thing.

I love Caskey for a million reasons, not the least of which is that she somehow puts up with me and all my craziness, but among those million reasons is this: Saying Yes is just a lot more fun than saying No. All of our lives together have been defined by the same thing that defines the work I've started to do: It's all about learning to take that leap of faith. Whether it's something monumental, like changing your life based on the flip of a coin—a story I'll get into a little later—or something tiny, like letting the last person who walked in the door decide what you're doing tonight. Everything begins by taking the part of you that has the false illusion of control and gently pushing it out the window, so that other part of you—the part that's willing to take the path that opens up in front of you—can begin to have some fun.

We found ourselves saying yes even before we knew what Ubi had in mind. Turns out what he had in mind sounded pretty interesting anyway: We were going to go to some kind of graffiti art show to benefit an artist who'd been stricken with Lou Gehrig's disease. I've always been a fan of graffiti art—I know a lot of people aren't, but I think it's a very real expression of very real feelings, done in a very real way. It's honest. It's a little crazy. And it's way outside the rules—all things I can respect and relate to.

The sun was going down over the palm trees of Venice, and the streets took on that beautiful and slightly sad glow that LA gets from the last glint of light bouncing back from the Pacific. The faint sounds of the Saturday night Venice Beach drum circle could be heard in the distance as we all crowded into my 1974 white-and-blue International Scout and headed to Culver City.

Ubi was the catalyst, the enzyme, the beginning of a chemical reaction that would change—well, everything.

♦

At the time, pop-up galleries, restaurants, and events were just finding their way to the emerging art district of Culver City. I knew by the location it would be cool, but I wasn't expecting what happened when we walked through the door: We were instantly transported by the graffiti—in space and time—to the grittiest downtown streets, to the underside of railroad trestles and the tops of warehouses and the sides of railroad cars.

It was a little strange, seeing all that graffiti out of its normal context, in big posters mounted on white walls—gigantic explosions of colors, huge names written in interlocking, three-dimensional, mind-bending shapes and blasts of pink and purple and green and black and red and a few hundred other colors that don't even have names, all coming at you at once.

The place was packed with hip-looking dudes and their beautiful girlfriends, all dressed to impress. Many of the men were artists who'd done pieces for this show. Ten of them had decorated three-foot-high spray-paint cans as characters with feet, each artist using his own distinct style. A palpable energy emanated from the room, from all these people, although their demeanor around people who were not of their group was sort of reserved. Their art, for the most part, is essentially illegal, so they're not used to having their faces associated with their art in public. A lot of kids, sixteen, seventeen years old, were running around with black books, getting the artists to sign them with their tags (although, to be accurate, graffiti isn't generally called "tagging"—that's associated with the gang side of graffiti art—when these famous LA artists at the show put their art up on a building or wherever, they call it "getting up"). Anyway, these kids were psyched, like they'd been let loose at a Grammys party—only they didn't give a damn about rock stars. To them, these artists were the stars, up close and personal and signing their books, and nothing could be better than that.

Caskey had a huge smile on her face, and she was staring at this one really colorful poster, high up on the wall in front of us. It was a copy of a graffiti artist's name, as he'd spray-painted it on walls in Los Angeles in the 1990s.

It took me a second to untangle the letters in my mind, but then I could read it:

Tempt.

Tempt One, it turns out, was something of a legend in Los Angeles. Each city, Rojelio had told us earlier, had its own kind of graffiti style. The old-fashioned New York subway-car "taggers," for example, were very different from the style of Mexican American graffiti artists known as "cholos"—originally a derisive term, now used as a matter of pride. Tempt was one of the first to fuse those styles into something new, something distinctly Los Angeles, and the graffiti artists who came after him treated him with enormous respect.

Ubi and Rojelio wandered over and caught us being caught up in the painting.

"Man," I said to him, "I'd really like to meet this artist. Is he here?"

Rojelio responded. "No, man," he said. "That's the guy with the ALS. That's the guy who this benefit is for."

I was blown away by that and took a step back, and for the first time noticed that someone had painted a portrait of Tempt in black and white, next to his graffiti. It was a surreal juxtaposition: in the portrait, Tempt was smiling and serene, but the contrast of his muted face in shades of gray, next to the vibrant colors that were so full of life, was haunting and a little painful.

I'd like to say I was moved to do something to help at that moment, but it wouldn't be true. There are so many times in life when the right thing to do taps you on the shoulder, but you don't turn around, you don't listen. You just sigh and move on. We spent a lot of time at the exhibit, talking to some of the artists and having them tell us about their pieces. In the end we bought one of the cans—a yellow spray-paint can created by the LA legend who goes by the name Slick; it had big red feet and a giant smile with a gold tooth.

When I got home, I went online to learn more about Tempt and found out he was just as significant a player as his fellow artists were making him out to be that night. He'd "gotten up" all over town—and not just on walls, but in museums as well. His art had been

An early piece of Tempt's artwork.

on display in the Museum of Contemporary Art in Los Angeles. I watched an interview with Tempt on video, on which he proudly and defiantly talked about graffiti art: "It's something that can't be tamed," he said. "It's wild and it's free, the very essence of the word 'freedom.'"

It was very sad to realize, as I watched him, that this significant voice had been silenced.

And then I got up from the kitchen counter where I usually check my email at night when everyone is in bed, closed the computer, put the sculpture on the mantel, and went upstairs to bed.

The next day, we woke up, and went about our lives.

Commit; Then Figure It Out

Our lives were pretty busy in the spring of 2007, when we went to the graffiti show. Six years before, we'd started our new company, The Ebeling Group. We call ourselves a Creative Task Force—part production company, part storytellers, part creative think tank. We'd had some success with commercials and graphics over the first few years, and won a bunch of awards for our creative design and outside-the-box thinking—and now business was really beginning to pick up.

The first big break came through MK12, one of the design collectives on my roster. These collectives were basically groups of graphic designers and animators, banded together under a single name in a company that was co-owned and operated by the founders themselves. I had about six of them at the time who worked with me exclusively. MK12 was contacted by Mark Forster, the director of a new film with Will Ferrell called *Stranger Than Fiction*, about a guy who slowly comes to realize that he's a character in someone else's book. Forster was trying to find a way to show that the main character, Harold Crick, an IRS auditor, had obsessive-compulsive disorder without coming right out and saying it or using any of the clichés you've seen in other movies. Forster's visual-effects supervisor had seen some other work MK12 had done and reached out to them.

MK12 came up with a brilliant new graphic design, what we call animated infographics, involving on-screen printouts of how many times Harold brushed his teeth, the precise directions he followed for tying his tie, and so on. They were clever but subtle; informative and scientific but very whimsical and fun.

We put together a little test reel, showing the graphic style and how we'd use it in the movie, and then went down to meet with Forster and his creative team. It was a pretty simple meeting: he walked in, we showed him the video a few times, we talked about it for a few minutes, he said, This is great, this is exactly what I'm looking for, and he walked out.

I was pleased, of course, but didn't think that much of it until I took a look at the faces of all the other folks in the room—the visual-effects supervisor, the producer, the editor, and the support staff were all looking around at each other, dumbfounded. They were silent for a while, and then one of them said, to no one in particular, "What the hell just happened?"

"What do you mean?" I asked. We'd never met with Forster before, so we had no idea why they were so stunned.

"Mark never approves anything like that," one of them responded. "He reviews things, he has long dialogues and conversations, he questions things—he never just says okay. You guys just nailed it. Your first pitch, and you hit a grand slam."

That was pretty cool to hear.

It was even cooler, after the movie came out, to hear the graphic arts community's positive response to the sequences in the film— and cooler still when other directors started seeking out the group behind the graphics. That film led to a lot of other very high-end work—we landed the title sequence for *Kite Runner* right after that, and that led to one of the crown jewels of the motion design world—the title sequence for the 007 film *Quantum of Solace*. Only four people and their companies have ever worked on those coveted iconic title sequences—only two of us are still living—so it's a pretty rare achievement. We ended up working on the graphics throughout the film, the video game, the DVD, and the music video—for which we were nominated for a Grammy. (I ended up taking my mom, my aunt, and my brother to the Grammys, since I had no idea when I would ever get there again. I figured taking Mom and Auntie Marilyn pretty much guarantees I can at least get a hall pass to purgatory at the end of this entire wild ride.)

So things were rolling right along. And yet, that fall, something was nagging at me. Some kind of unfinished business, sitting there in the corner, waiting for me to notice.

And I knew exactly what it was.

It was Tempt.

Something about that art exhibit had stuck with me. Especially that one painting—the juxtaposition of Tempt's name in those vibrant colors jumping off the wall, and that black-and-white portrait of his face, so serene, so peaceful, and yet so—absent. The portrait perfectly illustrated the fact that all these great and well-known graffiti artists were in that room, but this guy, who was one of the best of them, and the most well known, was not. His dad had been there, and his brother; I'd met them briefly, in passing, but we probably hadn't exchanged more than twenty words. Now, suddenly, I really wanted to talk to Tempt's dad again. And to do something for him. Or, more specifically, to help him do whatever he was trying to do for Tempt.

The family had set up the Tempt One Foundation to help defray the cost of his state-provided care. And so that Christmas, Caskey and I decided that instead of giving meaningless Christmas presents to our clients—a bottle of wine or a DVD box set of movies or whatever—we'd make a donation in their names. I arranged to meet with Tempt's dad.

It was the first of many meetings I'll never forget.

Although I'd assumed Tempt—whose real name is Tony—was Hispanic, his family is actually "Chino Latino"—his mother is Hispanic and his father, Ron Quan, is Chinese. Ron is an older guy who immediately puts you at ease; his hair is graying at the temples, and his well-worn face looks like he's been around the block a few times, but he has an easy smile and an earnest way that makes you feel that he's known you a long time even when you've just met. We'd arranged to meet at one of the oldest diners in LA. He was waiting outside when I got there, and held the door open and ushered me in. His other son, Steven, Tony's brother, was already sitting inside, drinking a cup of coffee. He's a few years younger than me, with a rock-star mane of hair. I introduced myself, and we just chatted for a while about everything and nothing—I'm not sure why it was taking me a while to get to the point. I mean, I'm the last guy in the world to be shy, but there was something about this moment that made me feel like I wanted to be careful and respectful. The more I heard about what they were going through, how hard it was for Tempt just to breathe, just to be fed, just to get the care and drugs and materials he needed to sustain his solitary, isolated existence—I just felt more and more humbled.

Finally, I got around to the point of the meeting. "So, we'd like to donate to the foundation," I said. "What is it you guys need? What are you going to use the money for?"

Ron started to answer, but Steven jumped in. "I just want to talk to my brother again," he said. "I just want to be able to communicate with him. That's our biggest problem."

This took me aback. I assumed there was some kind of Stephen Hawking–type box that they were able to use so Tempt could talk; if I had tried to guess the ten biggest problems they were having, communication wouldn't have been anywhere near the top of the list.

"How do you communicate with him now?" I asked. Steven started to explain. "We have a piece of paper that has the alphabet on it," he said. "We run our finger along that piece of paper, and when we get to the letter that Tempt wants, he blinks. We write down the letters, and letters become words, and words become sentences. It's hard, because sometimes he just blinks naturally, but we've kind of gotten to know the difference between his blinks, but still, it takes a long time just to get a word out. Sometimes he gets exhausted just finishing a short sentence."

We sat there silent, for a moment. I looked into Steven's eyes, and he looked into mine. I didn't know what kind of devices existed that might help Tempt, but I knew they were out there. I didn't know why he couldn't get one. But I did know what I had to do.

I had shown up with the desire to write a check. Instead, I ended up writing a check that I had no idea how I was going to cash.

"Okay, here's the deal," I said. "Tony's going to speak again. We're going to get him a machine, and he's going to speak again.

"And we're also going to figure out a way for him to do his art again. Because it's a travesty that someone who still has all of that in him isn't able to communicate it."

They were kind of stunned to hear me say that. Frankly, so was I. We talked a little while longer. "Do you know one of the last things that Tony said to me?" Ron said. "He said, 'I'm going to fight this disease. But I need a support team around me. And they have to believe that I'm not going to die.' That was the last memorable discussion I had with him, when he could still talk. And now . . ."

Ron gestured to me and smiled. I knew what he meant: that what I was doing was volunteering to be part of that team. Taking the leap of faith, of belief. And, in fact, that's exactly what I was doing.

I asked Ron and Steven not to say anything to Tempt just yet—I didn't want to build up hope until I had something concrete to offer. I don't believe in talking a big game. You do what you do, and you talk about it afterward. But still, it was a really high moment. I left that meeting invigorated and excited.

I was also scared to death, because I had no idea of how I was going to make good on what I had just committed to.

I mean, I had no medical experience, not much computer experience, and less than zero experience dealing with the medical community or the insurance community. And yet I was making a promise that I was going to succeed in those very worlds.

Now, I'm not going to harp on the "lessons" I've learned on this adventure. But this is one of those moments that I do think is worth thinking about, because it goes to the heart of everything that I'd learned up to this point, and everything I learned after.

I'm an adrenaline junkie. Motorcycles, hang gliding, snowboarding, you name it—those are the things that turn me on. As with surfing, there's something about the sense of danger that I love. A lot of people don't associate that sense with business, or at least with any sense of how a business plan should come together, but throughout my business life, there's always been an element of leaping before I look. While there isn't any one way to make a business succeed, that leap of faith is mine. As far as I'm concerned, you have to take that leap—that chance that you're going to fall flat on your face—if you're going to get over any hurdles worth passing.

Right now, you're probably facing some choices in your life, in your relationships, in your work, that are going to require you to make a decision. Go right, go left. Forge ahead, retreat. And you're weighing the ups and downs, and maybe even doing what sensible people do and making a list—drawing a line down a piece of paper and putting the pros on one side and the cons on another.

But what if you didn't?

What if you didn't weigh the cons? What if you didn't consider the what-ifs? What if you didn't consider what would happen if you failed? What if you didn't even allow for the possibility of failure?

Would that make you stupid? Or would that keep you focused and brave and alert and alive and aware?

Because every time I take a chance, roll the dice, make a commitment that I have no idea of how I'm going to keep, it's like the world opens up, and I'm at the very center of it. I never work harder, or smarter, or longer, or more intensely than when I have no clue of where the finish line is or how I'm going to reach it.

Say yes first, ask questions later. Commit, then figure it out.

You should try it sometime. It's good for the soul. And, more often than not, good for the business.

W. C. Fields, of all people, had a funny, absurd routine about this. He was trying to get somebody to do something crazy, and he made this argument:

"Take a chance. Take it while you're young. My uncle took a chance once. He jumped out of the basket of a hot-air balloon, and he took a chance of landing on a bale of hay.

"He didn't make it . . . but if he was a younger man, he would have! And that's the point. Don't wait too long in life."

Which makes no sense, of course.

And neither did me promising Tempt's father that I would get him a device to communicate with his son, and that his son would paint again.

But there I was. I had given myself no other choice but to get it done.

And sometimes, that's the only way to do it.

That day was the first time that the words, words I'd heard in another form, long ago, came to me; words that have become my mantra, not only through the process of helping Tempt, but through everything that came after:

If I don't do this, who will?

And if I don't do it now, then when will I do it?

Many times, over the next few years, I'd hear myself saying that: If not now, then when? If not me, then who?

It's hard to answer those questions by thinking of someone else's name or saying, "Some other time." Those questions beg you to answer with "Now" and "Me"—and to be scared to death after you do.

◆

My push to find a way for Tempt to communicate again started in earnest that Christmas. One of my employees, Blair Milbourne, helped me start on the research. We tripped across some fortuitous information right at the outset. A Swedish company called Tobii Technology, which was just a couple of years old, was growing by leaps and bounds, creating eye-tracking and eye-control functions in computer devices to help paralyzed people communicate, type, and so on. They were winning every award there was.

I thought, bingo! Well, that was easy. Now we just had to find somebody to pay for it.

Not so easy.

The MyTobii device—the one we needed for Tempt—was running north of $12,000. We talked to insurance companies, we talked to the state, we talked to charitable foundations—and we got nowhere, and the days stretched into weeks, and the weeks stretched into months, and we got nowhere.

I'll be honest: There were times that I thought of giving up. I mean, I think I spent more time on hold that year trying to convince someone, anyone, to step up to the plate than I had in my whole life—and you can't help but get frustrated and down when you're on hold for the same guy for the tenth time and you know his assistant is going to come on the line and tell you he's in a meeting and could you call back tomorrow.

It was starting to seem impossible. But I kept calling.

So what makes you call back that eleventh time? Well, it helps to be stubborn. And it helps to have an enormous amount of pent-up energy, which I always have an abundance of.

But something else was starting to form in my mind. The more the task started to seem impossible, the more the idea started to crystallize.

What if nothing is impossible?

What if you didn't give yourself the opportunity to fail?

What if the only limitations on what we do come from our own belief system, our own lack of faith in our ability? What if you start from the assumption, just for the hell of it, that all problems can be solved with the right people and the right tools and the right ideas, and that the only thing standing between you and those solutions is a lack of one of those three things?

Put aside for a second the question of whether you believe that. Imagine, just for the moment, what the world would feel like if it were true.

I'll tell you one thing that happens.

It makes you make that next call. And the next. And the next.

Because you never know.

It might not be true, after all, that nothing is impossible.

But then again, it just might.

◆

So I just kept calling, and had my staff keep calling, anyone we could get to pick up a phone. One way to keep yourself doing this is to figure out what part of the process you really, really enjoy and just focus on that. If you're an organizer, then focus on the organization. If you're a people person, focus on networking. Forget, for a moment, that there's a goal you might or might not get to: just focus on the doing of the thing.

For me, the fun part is the story. I'm a storyteller by trade and by avocation—I just love to tell stories. I mean, I'm having fun just telling you this story right now. And that's what I focused on. Whenever I could get anyone to listen, I'd launch into telling the story of Tempt, his art, his friends, his life; the aching sadness of how hard it is to communicate with his family, and how delightful and thrilling and exciting and wonderful it's going to be when—not if, but when—we get him the device that will let him speak. Think of the stories HE is going to tell!

It was the most exciting tale I'd ever told—and I'd try to get the other person on the phone to feel the excitement, too.

Just imagine, I'd tell them. What do you think it will be like once Tempt is allowed to speak?

◆

"In my personal experience, people treat you like you are invisible."

Tempt would write this later, about his long years of silence.

"When you are mute, the feelings of alienation and invisibility become magnified one thousand-fold."

Learning how to see behind that veil was so strange. On the one hand, Tony was a silent figure, lying in a hospital bed, a reclining Buddha, unmoving, being kept alive on a respirator. On the other hand, he was a vibrant, energetic artist named Tempt, a man who had transformed a particular kind of art in a way that inspired many others; an articulate, funny guy with a quick wit and a deep sense of compassion tinged with a sadness that never, not for a moment, bordered on self-pity.

I wanted so desperately to reunite Tony and Tempt: to let the silent man in the hospital bed communicate like the vital artist who was locked away inside.

And after four months, it happened.

"I think I got a bead on a machine that can really do what we need to do for Tempt," I told Ron over the phone. His response sent a chill through me: "Oh, that's great," he said. "I'll run it by him right away."

"Don't run anything by him yet!" I almost screamed into the phone. "Don't say anything until I know I can actually get it."

I was still insecure that I could make it happen, I guess—or maybe I just didn't want to disappoint Tempt. It's one thing to convince yourself that nothing is impossible—but I wasn't ready to let a guy who has spent years in a silent prison the size of a hospital bed pin his hopes to that belief.

And yet.

I really believed that we were going to make it happen.

◆

In the time that we were working on getting Tempt's machine, I got to know more about his background, mostly from his family. The story of his life before he was stricken with ALS—amyotrophic lateral sclerosis, also known as Lou Gehrig's disease. Tony was born in 1968, in South Central LA, a very tough part of town. His mother was working full-time as a secretary; his father had gone back to school to earn a business degree.

When Tony was about four or five, Ron took him to a playground. Ron was reading a newspaper on a bench, and little Tony was playing on one of those small round merry-go-rounds, those pieces of playground equipment that you sit on and spin around, when Ron noticed another young boy starting to yell at Tempt to get off it. Ron was perturbed to see a turf battle starting at such a young age, but he figured, well, he's going to have to learn to deal with it if he's going to live in this neighborhood. So he let the boys figure it out for themselves.

But that didn't work so well. The other boy punched Tony, who started to cry. Ron jumped up and rescued his son. He decided then and there that this sensitive boy didn't belong in this neighborhood.

They soon moved to a duplex in Monterey Park, a nicer neighborhood about ten miles east of Los Angeles. The family took one half of the duplex, and Ron moved his parents into the other half, so the boys—Steven was a baby at the time—would grow up around their extended family.

As they grew older, Tony and his friends shared the interests of most boys around that place and time—BMX bikes, breakdancing, skateboarding—but he didn't really show any interest in art until high school, when Ron started noticing drawings on all of Tony's notebooks. Tony stayed with it and later went to UC Santa Cruz to major in art. While he was there, Tony volunteered at a local rec center, teaching art to underprivileged youth.

Ron didn't know about Tony's interest in graffiti, however, until some of Tony's friends told him about it while Tony was away at college. Ron gave Tony a stern talking-to, admonishing him to focus on his books and his schoolwork ("Standard protocol from an Asian perspective," Ron said), but Tony kept sneaking off to practice his new craft, which was blossoming into full-fledged art. The first time Ron saw one of Tony's pieces was when Tony and a friend were commissioned to do a big mural in downtown LA. Ron was impressed by the work and secretly pleased at the Asian influence he saw in the mural.

But when Tony graduated, Ron's direction was clear: "Congratulations. Now go find work." ("That Asian perspective again," Ron said with a smile.)

Ron had a friend who knew someone at Disney Studios, who agreed to show Tony's portfolio to his boss. It was a great opening, and Ron kept bugging Tony to get his portfolio together, while Tony kept promising that it was almost done. But one day, Ron overheard Tony on the phone to a friend. "I will never work for a corporate structure," Tony said. "I will never be a slave in a corporate setting."

Ron confronted Tony, who apologized. "I'm sorry, Dad, but I want to work on my own magazine," the young man said. "Give me five years, and I promise I'll bring it to fruition."

Ron was furious—at first. But then, he thought back on his own youth.

As a teenager, Ron had a passion for the martial arts. His parents didn't approve, but Ron managed to create an entire mail order operation all on his own—selling paraphernalia, films on martial arts styles, weapons, uniforms, and so on. And one day when he was practicing martial arts in a park, some young boys came up to him and asked him to teach them what he was doing. He agreed to do it for free, but only if they agreed to work hard. That soon grew into the East Wind Foundation for Youth, which Ron started and which is still going to this day; it taught martial arts, as well as a folk dance from the villages of southern China called the South China Lion Dance. The dance was done to a big village drum, and when

Tony was old enough, he joined his father at the center and became an expert drummer.

So Ron knew a thing or two about following your passion and passing that passion on to your children. Ron also recognized that Tony's passion for teaching underprivileged children mirrored his own, and he was glad he had passed that on to his son.

So Ron agreed to let Tony live at home and work on the magazine—but beyond that, Tony had to support himself with odd jobs. Which he did. And the magazine started to take off. One day, Ron picked up a copy of the magazine and opened to the editorial page; he read a concise, persuasive editorial on some aspect of graffiti art. He looked at the writer's name—but didn't recognize it.

"This is really well written," Ron said. "Where did you find this writer?"

Tony looked up from what he was doing. "Oh, that's my pen name," he told his father. "That's me."

Ron realized, at that point, that Tony wasn't his son Tony anymore—he was his own man, who had his own talents and his own sense of values.

And the world around Tempt was beginning to sit up and take notice.

◆

During that long stretch when we were looking for a way to get a MyTobii for Tempt, I was also getting to know Tempt's graffiti-world friends. Caskey got to know them first, because we had decided to start documenting Tempt's story. We are, first and foremost, storytellers, and we knew that the story of Tempt—no matter how it turned out—would inspire others, just as it had already inspired us. We knew, instinctively, that the power of this tale was going to somehow stretch beyond Tempt, beyond us.

So Caskey took on the project: she would make the documentary, not only of the attempt to get Tempt to paint again, but also of the larger story, of who he is and all the people he affected. Which meant venturing off into the world of the graffiti artists.

At first, they didn't know what to make of Caskey, lugging her big camera across six-lane highways in the worst neighborhoods in town in the middle of the night, just to talk to them and ask them about Tempt. But persistence can give birth to trust, and the more she kept showing up, the more they began to trust her. And the more they heard about what we were trying to do for Tempt, the more they opened up.

They all wanted to talk about Tempt and the respect everyone had for him. The quotes that Caskey got on tape were nothing short of an homage to genius:

- "From my perspective, Tempt is the ultimate graffiti artist," said an artist named Defer.

- "You could see his command of balance, symmetry, style, space, form with his tags, his pieces," says an artist from New York, Mare139, who would become a good friend of ours.

- "He knew what to do with the Gothic letters, to make them strong and powerful and gangster. He put the muscle in it," Chaz Bojorquez said. "That's what I admire about Tempt. His letters were gorgeous."

Little by little, Caskey started piecing together what it was about Tempt that drew such praise, what made him unique. Clearly, he was infused by the spirit, the sense of freedom, that doing graffiti entails. Angst, an artist who was very close to Tempt, said he and Tempt had taken that adventure to new levels: "We were in places on the freeway that at the time nobody had been on," he said. "Like, nobody had set foot on since the time the freeway was constructed in the sixties."

A Tempt self-portrait.

But there was also something else about Tempt that drew the respect of those around him. While in college, still going by Tony, he had become something of a master in the ways of Native American spirituality, including the sweat lodge ceremony, which is central to Native American culture and spiritual life and a way of dedicating oneself to spiritual cleansing. It was part of Tempt's quest to live on a higher spiritual plane. Those around him noticed, respected, and admired it.

But beyond all else, was the art.

Tempt had quickly asserted himself as an artist with a sense of style that was at once old-school and thoroughly new. At one point Tempt was part of a couple of related crews called K2S and STN, who did graffiti art that they called Chino-Latino, which of course was Tempt's own heritage. "He brought the Latino aspect into it, but somehow that Asian crew, they still had that skill of hand more than anyone else," said Bojorquez. "Tempt was really the first one to approach calligraphy in a graffiti way."

Tempt had graduated from "bombing"—getting up on free-ways, a quick and dirty way of getting your graffiti out there—to "piecing"—painting with permission or in abandoned lots, where you could take several hours and really create masterpieces. And what masterpieces they were.

At the time, there was a lot of rivalry between the New York and Los Angeles graffiti scenes, with New York being the big badass crews and Los Angeles the snot-nosed little brother. But Tempt was changing all that, almost single-handedly. He was putting Los Angeles on the map. The New York artists respected, admired, appreciated, and even started to imitate what he was doing. Around that time, Tempt was also working on his graffiti-art magazine—called *Big Time*, it was the first magazine to really treat graffiti as a serious art form. And a lot of serious artists—and art galleries—took notice.

I've gotten a lot of blowback on supporting graffiti as an art. People ask me: Why are you spending all this time trying to help a guy who's basically vandalizing buildings and trains? Isn't that a criminal act in and of itself? And some people associate graffiti with gangs and criminals, which is largely a misperception. "Being in a gang is one thing," said Angst. "You grew up there, you had family that were gang members, you came up into that, and that's what it was. Doing graffiti, doing New York–style hip-hop graffiti, was another thing. They coexisted, but they were different worlds." Tempt himself, in an interview a few years earlier, compared graffiti to a more free-form style of music. "I see it a lot like jazz," he said. "John Coltrane playing with Miles Davis. They feed off each other in a certain communication that outsiders can't really understand. Fans can understand jazz to a certain extent, but never as deep as the artists who are communicating with each other."

I understand both sides of this argument, but, to me, there's no question that graffiti is an art form, one of the most important art forms of our day. Whether you agree or disagree on where that art is practiced, or how it's performed, almost everyone can see it as an incredible visual expression of honest thought and emotion through the medium of paint—as good a definition of art as I can muster. I've been to plenty of art shows where I saw art that was so horrendous that, if it were in a public space, I'd consider it vandalism. And I've been to many a graffiti wall that should have been in a gallery—and in fact, graffiti did start appearing in galleries. But you can't separate graffiti from the world it exists in. Look, if soldiers in World War II were painting "Kilroy was here" on the backs of their T-shirts as opposed to the sides of buildings, it wouldn't have carried the same message. When soldiers painted that wherever they went, they said to the enemy, and to the world, "Like it or not, we are here, and you have to deal with us." And that is the message, I think, of the graffiti artist who works in a public place.

There's an important distinction to draw between gang graffiti that was used to mark turf, and crews that guys like Tempt were part of. These crews were for kids who were into the art—in some sense, they were, for many kids, an escape from the gangs, "like joining a different Boys' Club," Rojelio told us. For them, it was all about the art. And for the artists, Tempt was a star.

Some graffiti artists had broken through and were working with clothing designers and making a decent living at it. But that's not what Tempt was about. "My art is and has always been focused entirely on the letter," Tempt wrote in an intro to an article in his magazine, back when he could still write. "Writers don't get up because they hope to get rich and all those other illusions. All this talk about portfolios, clothing lines, is nice, but it has nothing to do with writing. Writers write because for whatever reason it fills a void in their lives. It helps make sense of the world."

You don't have to agree with this view of graffiti as an essential form of urban expression. But Tempt was getting requests from art galleries all over the world. And the fact that this artist, who had left beautiful and powerful creations wherever he went, was suddenly silent, was a call to me. I was happy to let the world argue over whether graffiti was vandalism or public beautification or the expression of anti-authoritarian anger or just a bunch of kids with spray cans and time on their hands—that wasn't my argument to settle.

I had a MyTobii to find.

◆

As I've said, sometimes success is just a matter of not giving up. And finally, through sheer persistence, we annoyed enough people and got passed around to enough people that we finally landed on the phone with someone who was actually willing to listen. First, it was a wonderful woman named Dani Mohn at the Tobii company who took a real interest in finding just the right machine for Tempt. Then we managed—finally, finally—to get Medicaid to agree to pay for the damned thing.

Hallelujah.

The device, called the MyTobii P10, involved a big computer monitor on a long adjustable arm. There are lots of ways of accessing the device, but for Tempt, it involved a very sensitive camera that could "see" Tempt's eyes and track their movement. When they brought it in, Caskey was there, but I still felt that until I was sure I could deliver what I was trying to deliver, it wasn't my place to meet him yet. I heard later about what happened. At first, it was all business: the machine was adjusted to the proper height and distance, so that Tempt could see the screen, which displayed a yellow qwerty keyboard; as he moved his eyes, a small orange dot highlighted the letter he was "looking" at; if he gazed, or dwelled, on a letter long enough, that letter would register. Within minutes, he was forming words.

And sentences.

And ideas.

And thoughts.

And feelings.

And when he was done, the computer—in a robotic but clear voice—would speak what Tempt was saying.

And just like that, Buddha spoke. His first words in nearly eight years were: "Hey, this is awesome!"

◆

"When you're diagnosed with ALS, it's a traumatizing experience, because you're told you have only so long to live, and you will spend your time completely trapped inside a body that doesn't move anymore," Tempt wrote, shortly after that day. "Imagine having a mind that is totally intact and can still feel everything such as heat, cold, pain, and pleasure, but not being able to move or communicate for the rest of the time you are alive. It's a hard pill to swallow, and I was a total wreck for the first few weeks after I got the news. At this time I could still walk and talk, but everything was getting harder. I was deciding whether or not to commit suicide, while I still could. And I got angry and decided, if I had to go down, I wasn't going without a fight."

It was incredible to hear the eloquent and honest voice of a man whom I'd known only through his art—eloquent and honest art as well, but still, to hear what he was thinking, what he was feeling, what he was wanting to say all these years. The words came flowing out of him.

And they were beautiful.

As the days passed, he and his brother Steven finally got to have the talks they had been yearning for all those years. They talked about everything, and nothing. Their communicating took patience: Steven had to learn not to interrupt Tempt or try to finish his sentences for him. The machine would speak a word at a time, as Tempt wrote them, and there were long pauses between the words. When Tempt finished a sentence, the device would go back over each word and read the whole sentence in full.

When good friends like Rojelio—Angst, in the graffiti world—stopped by, they were even more amazed to be talking with Tempt.

"I was just completely flabbergasted," Rojelio said after one of those visits, where they had had the simple pleasure of talking over old friends and old times.

"Eva has a kid now, a baby," Rojelio told Tempt, catching Tempt up on an old crush of his. Tempt, in turn, wanted to know about Susan, an old girlfriend of Rojelio's.

"Is . . . She . . . Still . . . Back . . . East? Is she still back East?" the machine spoke.

"Susan, yeah, although they're thinking of moving back out here."

It seems like nothing, to hear the conversation now—and yet, try to imagine what it must have been like for Tempt, to have not been able to participate in that kind of simple give and take, year after year. And what it must have been like for his family and friends.

Soon Tempt was on the internet, chatting away with his old crew. "I was just stoked," his friend Slick told me. "I'm able to talk to my boy now on Facebook and email. We got our boy back! He may be confined to that bed, but on the internet we're all even again. You can see his sense of humor back—it's still Tempt, the Tempt I used to know."

It was great. Mind-blowing. Tempt was communicating again.

And yet, to those who knew him, as wonderful as this moment was, it was still a way station on the road to wherever we were going.

Because, to those who knew him, there was a greater need.

Tempt needed to do his art again.

Which meant I had a hell of a lot more work to do.

Shine Your Light

Now that Tempt had the MyTobii, his personality was shining through again, as if he'd been trapped and smothered under the sheets of that hospital bed for years and someone had finally ripped the covers off. He could communicate—and more than just communicate, he could talk and joke and argue and bust your chops. This astonishing change in his life gave everyone an incredible high. You could see it in the faces of his family, his friends, and his caretaker. And they told me you could see it in his eyes.

For me, getting the MyTobii for Tempt was an accomplishment, but really just a matter of logistics, no more, no less. I was long past thinking it was a big deal to turn a "no" into a "yes" when dealing with business people, or insurance companies, or banks, or whoever. It was always a matter of figuring out what their point of resistance was and finding my way around that, or under it, or through it. I can feel that in my bones. Some people call it determination, optimism, or a strong personality. It's really just what I do: Suss out people who really wanted to say "yes" but feel they have to say "no," and then present them the opportunity to take the "yes" path. Ultimately, people like saying yes way more than saying no. You just have to remind them. It's a matter of rechanneling or refocusing their energy in the yes direction.

And there are times when I am a relentless pit bull and such a pain in the ass that people say "yes" just to get me the hell out of their office or off the phone.

The promise I had made to Tempt's family—the promise that he would paint again—was gnawing at me. Because I knew that I would need more than blind optimism and willpower to create something that could really get him painting again and back into the art scene. The reality was, I had no idea how I was going to keep that promise. I only knew that I wasn't going to stop until I did.

To be honest, I can be pretty all-over-the-place. I'm better at juggling ten balls at once than I am at hitting a target with one of them. And in the next couple of months, I have to admit that I let other projects take over my attention. The promise to Tempt was sitting there, patiently, in a corner, waiting its turn, waiting for me to come up with an answer to an impossible question.

When I was a kid, I loved the puzzle about what happens when an unstoppable force meets an immovable object. Does the object move or not? If the force is unstoppable, then of course the object has to move—nothing can stop it.

But if the object is immovable, clearly it doesn't.

The answer lies in unraveling what's wrong with the question, as is so often the case. If there's an unstoppable force in the universe, then obviously there can be no immovable objects. And vice versa. If there are any objects that can't be moved, no matter what, then there can't be any truly unstoppable forces.

I mean, who are we to think anything is impossible? We evolved from primates who couldn't imagine what lay before them. There was a time when the printing press was inconceivable, circumnavigating the globe unthinkable, the steam engine unimaginable. These massive impossibilities became possible, then probable, then commonplace. So why should we challenge the inevitability of the possible?

So that's how I started feeling about the idea of the "impossible question." I really believe that there is an answer for everything. Whether we know that answer or not or can figure it out, that's another story. But in a universe where there's an answer for everything, then there are no impossible questions: there are only people like me, who don't know the answers yet.

The good thing about knowing that you don't know the answer—if you're honest about it—is that you're always on the lookout for people who are smarter than you. You just never know where you're going to find them.

◆

Several months had passed since Tempt got the MyTobii, and I was still nowhere on moving forward on my promise. The Ebeling Group was riding a big high, after scoring the James Bond movie title sequence, which had cemented our reputation for being at the top of our game. We were getting pretty well known internationally and operating internationally, too: we had offices in Toronto, New York, Rio, and Los Angeles, with satellite partner offices in South Africa, São Paulo, and Australia.

In March, I was asked to speak at a design conference in Greensboro, North Carolina. That day, I showed up on campus a little early with Ben Radatz of MK12, the group I worked with on the James Bond film; we were doing a presentation on those credits. A bunch of people were already hanging around in the orientation room, outside where the conference was going to be.

I spied these two guys who seemed interesting—animated and laughing and joking around—standing next to a big sign on a tripod that read, "Between the Lines: Innovation in Art, Architecture and Design." I sauntered over and introduced myself. Turns out they were from this outfit called the Graffiti Research Lab. GRL was a group dedicated, among other things, to helping graffiti artists find new ways to ply their trade. That was sort of what I was doing, in a one-paralyzed-artist-at-a-time kind of way, so we kind of bonded over that. We hung out and yakked our way through the afternoon.

The more I talked to these guys, the more I felt like they were kindred souls. For one thing, they weren't all about making money off their ventures. They were big proponents of what's known as "open source."

Originally, "open source" referred to computer programs where the source code would be made available to the public, so everyone could collaborate on revising and improving it. It's the opposite of the restrictive, hidden, proprietary code that became prevalent among big corporations. In that sense, open source was kind of the Occupy Wall Street of the internet. People who are proponents of open sourcing are all about leveling the playing field, making sure that opportunities are open to everybody, not just those who can afford to pay the entrance fee.

These guys "open-sourced" just about everything they invented—gave it away free, instructing anyone who was interested how to replicate what they'd done.

For example, they'd invented something called "LED Throwies"—a simple LED light, about the size of a big jellybean, attached to a powerful magnet; the devices came in a bunch of different colors. You could throw a few dozen up on a metal surface, creating a beautiful and thoroughly useless piece of art. Someone else might have just sold them online and made a mint, but these guys just put the instructions up on their website for anyone to copy, and moved on to the next project. They put the creativity and the fun ahead of the commerce, which is the pure essence of the artistic spirit.

One of the founders was Evan Roth, a quiet, intense-looking guy with a reddish goatee. If you want to know who Evan is, Google "badass motherfucker." I am not making that up. I mean that literally—when you Google it, the very first entry that comes up is "Evan Roth. The biggest Bad Ass Mother Fucker on the Internet . . . according to google." Somehow he figured out how to make that happen, and how to make it stick. I just checked it—it still works. That's the kind of guy he is. All the GRL guys seemed to do stuff like that just to do it. Just because they can. Or, more often, because someone told them that they can't.

If anyone could give Evan a run for his money on his biggest badass title, it was the other founder of GRL, James Powderly. James speaks with a kind of subtle drawl—kind of a deadpan monotone with a hint of a Jack Daniel's hangover—that belies his rebel spirit. Case in point: James went to China during the Olympics, planning to do some major art installation involving laser-light graffiti projected on a building. He was going to help out a group that was protesting the Chinese government's occupation of Tibet.

Somehow the government got wind of his plans and, after a while, he realized he was being followed. This was making him really paranoid. He was traveling in Communist China, and every time he turned around, the same woman was across the street, not saying anything, just watching him. It was like a scene out of a bad movie, only this was real.

A little too real. He went to meet his contacts at a restaurant to tell them that this was getting too scary and he was going to leave the country—but as he came out of the restaurant, the street exploded, a bunch of what appeared to be quiet old men sitting in chairs suddenly jumping up and turning out to be the police, more than two dozen cops with spotlights and video cameras, a huge spectacle of an arrest. They threw him and a dozen members of his group in the backs of some black SUVs and hauled them off to jail.

They were kept there for the entire Olympics, thirteen people crowded into a cell for eight, under what James called "nuanced horror" conditions: very little water, sleep deprivation, interrogation, the works. ("It was really gnarly," in his words). But one of his interrogators, he said, was an attractive Chinese woman who spoke good English; James, in his charismatic way, managed to make friends with her. By the end of the Olympics, he asked her to translate a phrase into Chinese and write it on a piece of paper in Chinese for him. He later got the phrase tattooed on his arm.

The phrase was, "I fought the law and the law won."

So that was James. Evan was no slouch, either: he told me about how, after 9/11, he had steel plates laser-etched with the phrases "What Are You Looking At?" and "Mind Your Own Business," and he'd put them in his carry-on luggage when he was traveling so the TSA agents would see them when the luggage went through the X-ray machine. They'd stop him and harass him, but then have to let him go because he hadn't done anything illegal.

I'd never met anyone like these guys.

I liked them a lot.

◆

James never got to do his laser-light art installation in China, but he was going to do it at this design conference. In fact, the very next night, everybody was invited to the main lawn to see James and Evan do their thing. The art concept that GRL had invented is called Laser Tag. It's not the game your kids play at the mall where they chase each other around a dark room with light-powered guns. James's version of Laser Tag involved actual tagging—as in, painting on buildings. I'd assumed they called their company Graffiti Research Lab as a kind of metaphor—I didn't realize they meant it literally, as well.

Imagine this: You have one of those laser pointers that shoots a tiny red light wherever you point it. Now imagine slowly running that light across a wall. Now imagine that instead of the light moving, it leaves a trail of light behind it—as if you'd brushed a laser paintbrush along the wall. Laser Tag works sort of like an Etch A Sketch—it's like painting in reverse—the surface of the Etch A Sketch is covered with some silver metallic stuff, and the stylus you're controlling is scraping away the coating wherever you move it. With *Laser Tag*, they project a black light across a huge surface (a building, a bridge, the Sphinx) and then with their laser, "erase" some of that black light to reveal a color, creating an effect that re-markably simulates graffiti—paint drips and all.

GRL began their presentation by talking about some of their

wilder escapades. They'd go to major tourist attractions, like the pyramids in Egypt, set up their laser printer, and let passersby write whatever they wanted. They put a huge "For Sale" sign on the Parthenon. Some of the projections would be political statements, telling off world leaders, but people would project anything: their phone numbers, "I Love You, Lisa," their ATM pin, for some reason. "And of course," said James, "a million penises."

As we stood in the courtyard in the cool darkness of the early evening, James and Evan started projecting some Laser Tags on a building at the far end of the lawn. They turned over the controls to the conference participants and got some interesting projections. "Copyright kills" got a rise from the crowd; some artistic participants managed to create a Pabst Blue Ribbon can, and the word *Oil* with oil dripping off of it; at one point, the police drove up and parked their car near the projection wall, and one of the participants drew the words "Hug Me" with an arrow pointing to the car. (And someone else changed that to "Oink.") Along with those kinds of projections, there were, of course, a bunch of penises.

James and Evan were mobbed afterward by folks who wanted to know more. And they could learn as much as they wanted, because the Laser Tag device was open-sourced, just like all their other creations. The operating specs for the laser tagger, and instructions for its assembly and use, are all online: you can go to their site right now, download it, and build one for yourself, if you have the time and inclination.

There is only one restriction to their open-sourcing of the Laser Tag. The last thing they wanted was for advertisers to get hold of this tool that is meant for artists, activists, and pranksters. They were delighted that lots of people had downloaded their info, and they were happy to help them out, but one of their main reasons for being was to even the playing field between big advertisers and the rest of the world—to allow regular folks to speak on the scale that advertisers could speak. So, a guy on their team named Theo Watson, their main software developer, came up with the solution. They included in the Laser Tag software a little subprogram that would detect whether a big advertising company had downloaded the program. If they did, then the next time they opened it, the company would get Rickrolled.

Rickrolling is one of those Internet memes. The way it works is, you click on a link for what you think is some relevant information, but it's a trick—the link really goes to the 1987 music video of Rick Astley singing "Never Gonna Give You Up." So that's what happened to the advertising companies—the GRL guys took great delight in seeing, on their website, that the companies were trying again and again to open the Laser Tag program, and just kept getting the Rick Astley video, until they finally just gave up.

As I said, I really liked these guys a lot. So the next day, when I was giving my own presentation, I was kind of disappointed that James and Evan didn't show to hear what I had to say. Until I found out where they were. Which I did, right in the middle of my presentation.

Somehow, they'd gotten access to the room next to the one in which I was doing my presentation—and they'd also gotten hold of two enormous speakers, like the ones you'd see at a concert. And right as I was giving my brilliant talk on all my brilliant work, I was interrupted by a blaring sound. To be precise, the blaring sound of Rick Astley, singing those inane, immortal lyrics, "Never gonna give you up, never gonna let you down . . ."

The audience was confused, and I wanted to explain it to them. But I couldn't stop laughing.

◆

I liked hanging with these guys, but a conference is a conference, and when it ended, there was a lot of talk about catching up again sometime (and some not-so-veiled threats of more Rickrolling when I least expected it), but that was about it.

When I got home, my wife, Caskey, had already put the boys to bed, so I went in and gave them a kiss in their sleep—there is nothing more peaceful than kissing your sleeping child, nothing that can bring you more into the moment, into your own life, than hearing that tiny snore and kissing that warm cheek, and pulling up the covers, and lingering in the doorway before you close it as quietly as you've ever closed a door.

So I was feeling pretty great as I sneaked back to the dining table. Caskey had made a big salad and a nice homey pot pie, and she'd waited to have dinner 'til I got there, and I'm sure she's sorry she did, because I just wouldn't shut up about the conference, and these guys I had met, and their laser tag schemes, how they created this software and made this machine that you could paint on buildings with, and how one of them had gone to jail in China over it. It must have been ten minutes before she could get a word in edgewise, and when she did, all she said was:

"Well, if you can control the laser painter with a mouse, why couldn't Tempt control it with his MyTobii? Why couldn't he paint with that?"

It was the simplest, most obvious, brilliant solution, sitting there, right in front of us. I was dumbfounded. I hadn't even been thinking about Tempt, to be honest. And I hadn't even thought for a second of connecting Tempt's talking device, which he controlled with his eyes, to the laser device—but of course, there had to be a way. It was the answer we had been looking for, for six months.

"Honey," Caskey said, "would you pass me the salad dressing?"

◆

We jabbered away for the next hour or so, figuring out how this would work.

The next day, I called James and Evan. I told them about the project and asked if they'd come to LA to help.

And I was shocked when they said no.

They said no because our original idea was to build something with the MyTobii, that machine that Tempt was using to communicate with. And MyTobii was a corporation. These guys were true to their core—they didn't want to build something that some big corporation was going to get the credit for. It just wasn't in their DNA.

While I understood their ethics, I was beyond disappointed, because I just wanted Tempt to draw again. Period. I thought we had finally cracked the code, but the code crackers themselves were the ones saying no. I wanted to force the matter, but for once I kept my mouth shut and just said, "Well, let's think about it and get back in touch in a week or so."

Turned out, they didn't need a week or so.

Two days later, they called back. First, it was James, then Evan. They had turned 180 degrees—not only were they saying yes, they were saying it emphatically.

They just had one condition—one that would come to shape every decision that came afterward.

Why do we need the MyTobii device, they asked? Why can't we just build something the eye can write with—and draw with— ourselves? We could build an "eye-writing" device ourselves, from scratch, and put it out there open source. They wanted to help Tempt, of course, but they also wanted this to be an adventure that helped advance the story of Open Source and the Do It Yourself philosophy.

It was a great idea. And it became part of the core philosophy that launched us on our way.

Jump and the Net Will Appear

The next couple of months were a blur, because now we were talking not just about hooking two machines up to each other, but actually creating an eye-writing device that anyone could use and afford. Between Caskey, me, and the GRL guys, we knew all the folks we'd need. A team of seven in all, each one a master at one aspect of what we needed to do. Our plan was to fly everybody to Los Angeles to work on the thing together—no mean feat, seeing as how they were scattered all around the globe, from Germany to Spain, China to the Netherlands, Utah to New York—and back again. The cost was going to be pretty steep. Then Caskey said that if we could just get everyone here, we could put them all up at the house and cook for them for the next ten days they'd be here—so the only cost would be the airfare.

God bless Caskey.

When you have that many travel and creative logistics to work out, you can't think about how impossible it is, you just have to keep hacking away at it until it's done. Every Skype call led to a flurry of emails, every email to another conference call. We talked about ocular recognition, about how to build the hardware for our eye-tracking device, how to write the software, what existed in the open-source world, and what we would have to come up with on our own. It took several months, but finally, we had things lined up.

April 1, 2009, was one of those perfect Los Angeles days when the air just tells you that everything's going to be all right. I spent the day shuttling back and forth to the airport in a beautiful boat of a car we had, a canary yellow 1964 Buick Wildcat convertible.

A guy named Theo Watson, an expert in interactive environments, was the first to arrive, traveling from Amsterdam—a sweet, soft-spoken, understated guy (three adjectives you wouldn't use to describe the rest of the crew). It was like he was the front man for the revolution. James came next, from Berlin, followed by the rest of the crew: Evan Roth from Beijing; an ocular reading specialist, a woman named Chris Sugrue, from Spain; Zach Lieberman from New York; and an über-hacker-programmer-comedian who went by the name Love Monkey, who flew himself in because he was such a huge believer in the project. You never felt so much brain power in one room—with constant hip-hop accompaniment.

Everybody was psyched about the project. The moment they got into the car, they wanted to know everything: How Tempt was doing, what he knew about the project (which was still nothing, by the way. I'd requested that his family try not to say anything to him. I still didn't want to promise him anything until I knew I could deliver it). Everyone had come up with ideas for getting this thing done—and were talking over each other to get the ideas out.

Even before we got to the house—just on those shuttle rides from the airport—a plan started to take shape. For one, we agreed on a name for the gizmo we were trying to invent: the EyeWriter. We had already come up with what the EyeWriter would look like and how it would generally work: We would get some cheap sunglasses on the boardwalk and attach two webcams to them that could see the wearer's eyes. We'd have to come up with some ocular-recognition software, so that as the camera tracked the eye's movements, a program could translate those into the movement of a cursor, or more specifically, simulate the movements and functions of a mouse. We decided to use the "blink" function to register a letter—to have Tempt blink, rather than just gaze, to register the letter he wanted. Then, we had to create the painting program itself. This would turn out to be one of the most important parts of the project. Once the cursor was moving, we had to figure out how to translate that movement into actually painting. How you would "pick up" the paintbrush, put it down again, change colors, and so on. And finally, we had to work out the interface—how that painting program would communicate with the Laser Tag device.

How hard could that be?

Within a few hours everyone had arrived, and our house was humming with activity—I'd set up two long tables to work on, and guys just dropped their backpacks, unpacked the huge projectors and other equipment they'd hauled along, and got right to work, scribbling drawings on art pads, laughing at each other's jokes, and blaring A Tribe Called Quest like they owned the place.

Which they kind of did.

Caskey and the boys and I had given up the house to the project gang and moved into a little bungalow in the back. A bunch of houses like ours in Venice and Santa Monica have little bungalows; it's an artsy community, and a lot of folks use them for artist's shacks. Ours had become more of a work and storage area, but it helped to have a kind of firewall between the family and the seven-nation army. Not that it was bad for the boys to be around such brilliant creative people—far from it. I will say that these were not family guys, and they didn't exactly know what's appropriate to say around children, and said some weird things like, "Hey little man, one day when you grow up you'll understand that the world is an evil place." And I'm like, "Um, son, can you just erase that from your memory, please, or at least write it down so I can give it to your shrink when you grow up?" But for the most part, I was thrilled to have my boys in the midst of the whole scene and thrilled that they enjoyed it. I think that exposing kids to the creative process—the real, honest, frenetic creative process—early on, in an intense way, has to have an impact later on. I sure hope so, anyway.

The sense of excitement and creativity was palpable. You could hear it, you could see it, you could taste it. There is a freedom that comes with a thoroughly creative, thoroughly out-there project. Letting your mind be free enough to come up with solutions everyone else thought were impossible makes you act free in all sorts of other ways as well, like sleeping until noon and working 'til dawn, trying to see if you can bicycle while sitting on the seat backwards, or drawing on your desktop for three hours with no real goal in mind. When you free your mind and act a little more out there, you allow the creative process to begin.

We had all our meals together, one and all: that first night I cooked enough pasta to feed the Los Angeles Dodgers (feeding the creative process seemed to involve massive amounts of food and beer). The gang sat around the table, telling their tales and catching up on each other's escapades.

If you've never broken bread with someone who knows what it takes to sit in a parking lot outside the bank and electronically read your ATM card while you're withdrawing twenty bucks, let me tell you, it's a strange experience.

So that first day was a revelation: it was noisy, it was funny, it was intense.

And it was working.

As free-spirited as these guys were, they were that dedicated. And that good. By evening the work was proceeding in earnest. Everybody had their assigned roles—or, to be more specific, everybody had something they were good at, and all their talents fit together like a jigsaw puzzle. James and Evan, basically the leaders of this leaderless band of geniuses, were the fabricators—they could take apart a webcam and rewire it or weld copper wire onto a plastic sunglass frame. Love Monkey had a knack for taking things apart and putting them back together in a creative, different way. Theo, Chris, and Zach were the programmers: they were doing the hard coding. And when I say hard, I mean hard.

Ocular recognition software is no walk in the park. The team had to figure out ways for the camera to recognize the pupil, which is not easy in and of itself. We tried illuminating the eye to create better contrast, but that proved way too cumbersome; so we tried tweaking the contrast in the computer itself, sort of the way you'd adjust the contrast and brightness of a photo when you're editing in Photoshop. Then we had to calibrate the program so that it detected the tiniest eye movement. We also had to take into account that the eye is round, not flat, and yet the artist is painting on a flat plane—at this point, a computer screen. It's the same problem you'd have in making a map of the earth. If you don't compensate for the roundness of the surface you're scanning, then the parts by the poles get distorted (which is why everybody thinks Alaska is bigger than Mexico, or that Greenland is twice as big as both of them).

So the programmers set up a grid system on their screens to register the eye movements as recorded by the webcams, and I ran back and forth to Home Depot to get copper wire or plastic tubing or a hundred other things everybody needed. A couple of the guys jumped on bicycles and rode down to the boardwalk to buy a bunch of sunglasses for the EyeWriter's frame—we were going to punch out the glass and rig the cameras on them. Of course, GRL being GRL, they couldn't choose the sunglasses just on the basis of which ones would work the best—they had to be ironic, too. They first got some Kanye West–shades, the ones with the little slats across them like venetian blinds. In the end they settled on a simpler pair of plastic frames. With the lenses punched out, they looked like those fake Groucho Marx glasses that kids used to wear on Halloween.

And lo and behold, it all started coming together. After just one day, they had a working prototype.

It was a bulky, clumsy thing. Attached to the front were the lenses of two webcams they'd taken apart; plastic tubing, attached with copper wires and plastic wire ties, ran from the lenses to the back of the right earpiece, carrying the wires that transmitted the images from the cameras to a laptop on the desk.

James tried on the prototype first. He looked like a character out of a science fiction movie, but this was "science fact": the cameras actually picked up his eye movements and tracked them on a computer screen. The guys had written a simple program: the left-eye camera was like a mouse button. It just detected whether that eye was open or closed. Closed meant "on." When the left eye was closed, that was a signal for the second camera to detect movement in the right eye and begin drawing. When the left eye was open, that was like lifting your pen up from the paper—you could use your right-eye movement to move the cursor to the place you wanted to start your next letter, close the left eye, and start drawing again.

In theory, anyway.

James put the glasses on, and we all crowded around behind him. For the first time since everyone arrived, no one was talking. The room got quiet, except for the constant beat of the hip-hop music. Appropriately, someone had cued up a song by Bone Thugs-n-Harmony, and as the phrase "look into my eyes and tell me what it is you see" boomed out of the speakers, the cameras followed James's right eye, and we all stared at the screen.

And quickly, if somewhat roughly, the cursor started to move. And it drew a perfectly recognizable, square-edged, letter *G*.

The silence broke immediately, and everyone was talking at once. Cursing, mostly. "Fuck yes!" and "That is fucking awesome!" seemed to be the prevailing sentiments. They didn't seem to notice, or care, that my kids were around. Frankly, if one of my kids turns out to have a sailor mouth but be as brilliant as the talent that had assembled in my living room and kitchen, that's okay with me.

It was a surreal moment. Caskey and I had talked about this for almost two years, ever since we'd gone to the graffiti art exhibit. And when you talk about something for that long, there's a part of you that is skeptical. Disbelieving. A part of you that just thinks, well, talk all you want, mister, but this ain't really gonna happen.

The art of getting things done begins with overcoming that voice.

Let's be clear. When I talk about overcoming that voice, I'm not talking about ignoring it or pretending it doesn't exist. I am not fearless. I fear failure. And I fear failure a lot. But I teach this to my boys: When you're feeling afraid of something, or afraid you can't do something, don't deny that fear. Don't just pretend it doesn't exist. Allow it in. Say hello to it. Get to know it.

And then kick it in the ass and move on.

I believe I can do what I set my mind to—so maybe I'm adept at blocking out that voice, once I've decided to move on—but it's not like I don't experience it. It's more a matter of how much power I allow it to have. The disbelieving part of me, the voice of doubt, is sitting there in the corner, quiet and patient, waiting for me to fail, muttering under its breath, "You can't do it. It's impossible." There just comes that point at which you do have to ignore it, and go and do what needs to be done.

And then, when the impossible thing gets done—when you actually see it happen with your own eyes—you can finally face that disbelieving, critical part of you.

You can look it right in the eye.

And say, shut the hell up.

◆

We continued to refine the EyeWriter over the next couple of days. We had been using a simple Sony PS3 webcam, but the contrast just wasn't good enough to register the movement as finely as we needed to. So we went back to the idea of illuminating the pupil. We attached three tiny infrared LED lights to the glasses, and that did the trick.

By the fourth prototype, we had something working a lot better than the first one: better tracking of the eye, a better way to register blinks, smoother movement of the cursor, a bit lighter. I still had not made any direct contact with Tempt—I know he was emailing with friends and family a lot, using the MyTobii, but I didn't think it was my place to jump in.

One thing he expressed, at one point, was echoing around in my head: "Prior to my paralysis," he had said, "I felt a profound sense of fulfillment being of service to the community. The loss of that, coupled with the loss of my ability to paint and draw, left me with a sense of emptiness." The pride and the pain contained in that thought were inspiring and a little frightening. Getting Tempt to paint again was important on a level like nothing I had ever done.

Tempt's father and brother had, finally, let him know that the ragtag army was in town working on this project, and that the day was getting close to try it out. Word got back that Tempt was very excited. He wanted this project to work. He wanted to do his art again.

And on Sunday, April 5, 2009, it was showtime.

The entire crew came with me to the hospital. I wanted to go in first, so they waited outside. I will admit that I was kind of nervous.

First off, I hate hospitals. When my dad was dying and I would go see him, I developed that deep-seated aversion to hospitals from the smell of urine and antiseptics locked in eternal battle, the surreal fluorescent lights that make even the healthy visitors look as sick as the patients, the self-absorbed doctors walking quickly and never making eye contact, the signs alerting you to the dangers of sharp objects. The forced smiles on the faces of the receptionists and the nurses, the clipped tones they spoke in, the measured way they didn't quite answer direct questions, all led to a sense of impending doom. So I come across my hatred of hospitals honestly, and the ward that Tony was on was an especially difficult place to be. Most of the people there are on life support and have no control over their bodies. You can walk down the hall past fifty rooms, all with the doors open, all with people on ventilators.

But as I stood in that hallway outside Tempt's room, I was also nervous like a kid on a first date with a girl he's been secretly admiring for years. Waiting this long to meet Tempt had infused the moment with a little more energy than I'd expected.

But what the hell. Can't stand in the hallway forever. In hospitals, as in life.

◆

When I first walked into the room, I was overwhelmed by the sounds and the sights: hoses and monitors and tubes everywhere, a constant slow beeping, and the lung machine making Tempt breathe, making that sucking, suctioning sound, like an old man wheezing for breath, and then quietly shushing the air back out, like the machine was telling you to be quiet and listen for the next wheeze. A quick metallic click, and the process repeated itself, hypnotically, and not a little frighteningly. It was accompanied by another suctioning sound, pulling the saliva from Tempt's mouth, and I looked up from there into his eyes.

And they were smiling at me.

It's amazing, considering that the rest of his face was paralyzed, but he was able to convey so much emotion with just his eyes. They were happy, and excited, and kind, all at the same time. I don't know how long I had been staring at the tubes and the machines; I hoped it wasn't too long, and I started for a second to feel embarrassed about that. But the embarrassment fell away when he saw me catch his eye, and he raised his eyebrows in a little gesture of hello.

It was also quite amazing, for a guy who's paralyzed and basically helpless in a bed, how much dignity and grace he conveyed. Though I had seen many pictures of him, I wasn't quite prepared for the power of his personality that came through when in the same room, even immobilized as he was: his almost Native American features, his high prominent forehead, a face smooth and symmetrical but with the squat nose of a fighter. He had dark eyebrows and, whether by chance or design, a little hint of a mustache and goatee.

"Hey, man, nice to finally meet you," I managed to say.

"Nice. . . ." I heard from the MyTobii. It took me a second to realize that it was Tempt, talking through the machine. It was slow, but not terribly so; I cautioned myself not to interrupt, just to wait patiently for him to talk, in his own way.

"To . . . Meet . . . You . . . As . . . Well . . ."

I thought that was the end of it and I was about to say something else, but he added one more word:

" . . . Dude."

And at that, we began chatting away like nothing unusual was happening here. I'm pretty reserved, and I'd learn soon enough that he was as well, so we didn't make a big deal of what was clearly a big moment for both of us. We just slipped into the business of the day. I'd decided I wasn't gonna meet this guy until I could deliver the goods. Well, now I had the goods with me, waiting with my posse right outside the door. I was eager to get to it.

I guess Tempt was, too.

I brought in James and Evan; I could tell that Tempt liked that they seemed to be from his world, not straitlaced computer-nerd types.

"Man, we're just big fans of your work," James was saying. "We think what you've done is amazing, and we just wanna see you get back to it."

They waited a moment—we had coached each other not to prattle on too much, to give Tempt a chance to respond. Sure enough, his eyes had turned to the MyTobii, and a second later, the mechanical voice came out.

"Rock . . . on."

That cracked us all up. James showed Tempt the glasses, and Tempt looked over at his talking machine and a second later we heard, "Those . . . Are . . . Pretty . . . Dope." It was stunning, really, to see that Tempt—that paralyzed guy in a bed—was trying to make everyone comfortable. And succeeding.

From there it was all business. James fit the EyeWriter onto Tempt's head and explained how it would work—how he'd use a blink to "click" the mouse and how to start drawing a line as the

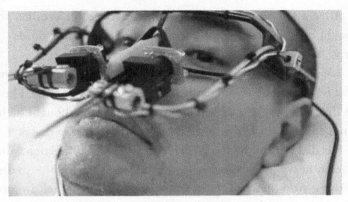

Tempt tries on the EyeWriter for the first time.

cursor followed his eye movements, and how to blink again to "lift" the pen off the paper (or the cursor off the screen, to be precise).

Then we had to move the MyTobii out of the way to get our system in place, so Tempt couldn't communicate with us, and I panicked for a second. What if we're hurting him? What if we're suffocating him? How could he let us know? But I looked at his eyes again, and there was no panic, no worry—he was taking in all that was happening, and he was intensely focused on what would come next.

His brother had moved close with the old-fashioned page of letters that he'd run his fingers along, in case Tempt did need to talk to us, but some silent communication passed between them. Tempt was saying, relax, my brother. I got this.

Tempt was going to draw on the computer monitor; we were projecting what he drew onto a big screen on the wall, but he couldn't see that and draw at the same time. An electric charge ran through us all when he began to draw with his eyes. But then he stopped. He'd managed just the most rudimentary scrawl, barely a single scribble. The device clearly wasn't tracking correctly. It was a success, because we proved that the concept would work, but no one was feeling enormously successful. We were feeling pretty crappy, to be honest.

After a few minutes, Tempt looked over to his brother, who brought over the letter chart. He blinked out just a few words: "It's heavy," he said, and then, just, "Tired."

We took the EyeWriter off him. Tempt looked over to me, and I swear he had a look of sympathy in his eyes. Like, hey, man, I know you did your best. He looked almost as though he thought he had let me down, but I felt we were the ones who'd let him down.

His dad put on the EyeWriter, and said, "Yeah, he's right, these are really heavy." We'd spent so much time figuring out how to make the thing work, we hadn't considered how it would feel. Immediately, ideas started popping around: we could replace the copper tubing with aluminum, we could lighten some of the wires.

And then James asked a question that would change everything.

"Are we sure," he said, "that we need two cameras?"

◆

The next couple of days were a frantic, manic hustle. That simple idea—that we could do this with one camera—was like a shot of adrenaline. Of course! Both of your eyes move together. So the movement of one eye was all the camera needed to track. We were using the second camera mainly to record an eye blink—turning the cursor on or off—but we realized we could set it up so that Tempt could communicate with the device by blinking one eye to select a "pen," and blinking again. We told the program to just wait a few seconds after that second blink and before telling the cursor to engage. That would give Tempt time to move the cursor to the place he wanted to start his next line, and then—as the cursor engaged—start painting. A blink of the same eye lifted the pen, and he could start the process again.

So some of the guys were up all night, writing new code to make the EyeWriter track better, trying to figure out how to squeeze a few tenths of an ounce more out of the superstructure, seeing how little light we could get away with and still get the contrast we needed. I was doing what I do best—set everything up, stand back, and let the mad scientists be mad.

Part of getting things done is knowing when you yourself are not the guy getting things done. A lot of managers need to feel like they're in the center of everything, and they screw up the works because of their need to see their own fingerprints. But success comes from building structures that stand on their own, not structures that require you to lean against them in order to prop them up. I found the right people. I motivated them. I set the task in front of them. And then I stepped back. I can't write algorithms like the computer guys, I can't fabricate like the builders, and I sure can't put the whole system together like this team of crazies can. So over the next few days, I did what they needed me to do: make pancakes and pasta, buy beer and cigarettes, make a hundred runs to Radio Shack and Home Depot, and let them do their jobs.

The night after our first failed attempt, we were back in Tempt's hospital room. The night before had been very draining for him— not just physically, but emotionally. He had lived in a silent room, a silent world, for many years; to suddenly have a ragtag army of hackers jabbering away, and Caskey and her team filming the whole thing, was overwhelming. So this second night, we were determined to be more efficient—get in, do our trial, get the heck out.

The second trial went better than the first; we could see it was taking an enormous effort on Tempt's part. But sure enough, there on his tablet, and on the projection on the sheet we'd hung on the wall, was a shaky, but distinct, letter *T*. It wasn't art; he wasn't drawing, by any means; but we were getting there.

That night we were all business, talking logistics, setting up a schedule, trying to get out as quickly as we could. But as we were leaving, after they'd put the MyTobii back in place, we heard the machine's mechanical white-guy-robot voice speaking what Tempt wanted to tell us:

"Sorry . . . Guys. I . . . Was . . . Hoping . . . To . . . Bust . . . You . . . Some . . . Fly . . . Styles . . . By . . . Now."

◆

Ten days fly by like ten minutes when you're trying to do what seems impossible. The team of seven had round-trip nonrefundable tickets, and their departure date was zooming closer. Tempt still hadn't written his full name yet, let alone drawn it in any artistic way. We'd changed the EyeWriter so that he could look at the big sheet that was hanging on the wall as he was drawing. That helped—just conceptually, drawing a line on a wide canvas is easier and more forgiving than trying to do it on a little screen. Imagine painting on a grain of rice versus painting on a wall—any tiny fluctuations in your movement will be exaggerated on the small canvas but not noticed on the larger one. So painting on the big canvas helped.

We had to schedule the big attempt at Laser Tagging the building across the street, even though we didn't know for sure whether it was going to work. But learning to jump first and assume that the net will appear is built on getting beyond the fear of failure. We all believed it was going to work. And you can follow that belief, or you can follow the fear.

Guess which we do.

In fact, we did more than gamble that it would work—we went all in. People say, if you want to get your housework done, invite all your friends to dinner, and it'll get done. So that's what we did: we invited everyone we knew and every one of Tempt's crew.

The night of the big attempt, a huge crowd was on hand. Part of our team was up in Tempt's room. Another group set up the projector on the roof of a car dealership nearby. The best vantage point for watching the projection was from a parking lot across the street, so we broke into it, as was our style; I guess we could have tried to get permission, but that just didn't feel right.

It's easier to get forgiveness than permission, but you get a lot more done if you don't feel like you need either of those things.

Besides, if we had asked to use the parking lot and been turned down, then we really couldn't have done the demo. Since we didn't ask, we weren't technically doing something anyone had told us not to. Such is the logic of the graffiti artist. And the hacker. And me.

All of Tempt's graffiti-artist friends—Slick, Defer, Prime, Duke, and Angst—were down in the parking lot, giving an air of authenticity to the whole scene. It was very cool: his old world of graffiti artists was meeting his new world of Laser Tag hackers. Everyone was stoked.

We moved Tempt's bed to the side of the room, so he could see out the window and get a sense of the scope of how big his painting would be. He'd seen videos of the Laser Tag device, knew how cool it was, and was excited about being the one to put it into action with the EyeWriter. He would follow the progress of the drawings he did on the sheet that was hanging on his room, just as he had been doing. Then, with a blink, he could pause the process, look out the window, and see what he had drawn projected in lights thirty feet high.

I was confident that something would come out of this—some art, some justification for all this effort, some positive result, some proof that nothing was impossible. And so we went about setting up the device in his room, with a wireless signal sent through a LAN—a local access network—we'd set up to transmit to the Laser Tag device on the car dealership roof.

And the wireless signal didn't work.

You don't need a MyTobii to hear what all of us were thinking, and unable to say out loud.

Oh . . . crap.

So it was seven at night, and I knew all the stores were about to close and, like a madman, I went careening down the streets of Alhambra in that boat of a yellow Buick, from the AT&T store to the T-Mobile store to the Radio Shack, buying up every wireless card, hoping that at least one of them would work.

The last one I bought was the Sprint card—which would turn out to be the one that worked—but I almost had a brain aneurism buying it.

"Here," I said to the clerk at the counter and tossed the card down. The young kid had a name tag I was too crazed to read. I was out of breath and sweating bullets. "I just need this."

"Okay, sir," the kid responded. "Now with our wireless card, you can sign up for any of our Sprint wireless plans. We recommend the Platinum Plan, which comes with—"

I interrupted him sternly, with just a feeble attempt at politeness, "Yeah, I don't need the plan. I'm just going to hack the card to set up a LAN. So just the card, thanks."

The kid was unfazed. "Yes, sir," he said. "But you do realize that with the Platinum Plan—"

"Just the card. Just the card. Just the card. Nothing else. No plan. Just the card," I said, feeling on the verge of going postal. I was being one of those rude people whom I usually hate, but I had no patience left. If the kid said anything other than "You can slide your credit card now," I was either going to run out of the store with the card or start smashing stuff.

Fortunately, the kid gave up on selling me the Platinum Plan and cashed me out. I mumbled a perfunctory, "Sorry, dude." I wanted to explain, but there was no time.

I got back and tossed the cards to the guys in the room, who took about five seconds to figure out which one would work and set it up. We heard a faint cheer come up from the parking lot, so we knew we were back in business.

Through this all, Tempt had that Zen Buddha peaceful air about him, that thousand-year patience; if he was worried about all the hubbub, he didn't show it. He was the on-deck batter, taking his practice swings, knowing that at some point he would get to step up to the plate, and he would be ready.

By now I had gotten my cool back. I locked eyes with Tempt just for a second, wished him luck, and headed down to the parking lot to join Caskey and the kids, along with everyone else. It was like a party was going on. Lance, my brother (and best friend), had driven up from

San Diego, but this was the first time I'd seen him there, and we grabbed each other and pounded our fists into each other's backs, and I told him, this is going to be good. Really good. Tempt's graffiti compadres were all gathered, and some music was playing, and people were messing around with the Laser Tag machine, throwing some writing up on the walls.

And the real party was just about to start.

We were on cell phones with the guys back in the room, and when they gave me the signal, I made the announcement.

"Okay, everybody, can I have your attention?" It took the crowd a minute to quiet down, but little by little everybody got that what they'd come for was about to happen.

"The next thing you see go up on that wall," I said, "will be drawn by Tempt."

No one spoke. No one moved. All eyes were on the building across the street.

The yellow light started to move, horizontally at first, and then down, forming a big, slightly cartoonish, definitely stylish, block letter *T*. And then, before our eyes, faster than we could have hoped for, and more beautiful than we could have imagined, it emerged, a little shaky perhaps, but nevertheless a strong and streetwise graffiti drawing of the name.

Tempt.

Suddenly, as if they were one person, the crowd began to roar. People were hugging and high-fiving and continuing to cheer. I kept looking back up, to make sure it was really there. And there it was. Bright as day and proud as the street.

Tempt.

◆

"That was the first time I'd drawn anything since 2003," Tempt said afterward, through the MyTobii. "I felt like I had been held underwater, and someone finally reached down and pulled my head up so I could take a breath." Awesome. "I am going to take a couple of more stabs at it," Tempt said, "after catching some Z's. If I wasn't so tired I'd have spent all day goofing around and tagging."

I don't know why we're here, on this Earth. I know it's not to make money. I know it's not to just have fun, although challenging myself to take the harder course on the mountain, the harder mountain bike trail, feeds my adrenaline addiction. But this project for Tempt was about more than the adrenaline rush.

In my view, we're all rickety little boats, motoring across the narrow expanse of time that we have here. If you're going to be successful, you need to leave a wake behind you. If you go slow and don't leave a wake, then what's the point? And if you have kids, it's twice as important to make waves, because you don't just want to leave a legacy on your own, you want to show them—by example—how to leave a legacy for themselves, too. So when it's their turn, they'll leave a wake, as well. I mean, they're going to go through enough therapy for the bad stuff you taught them. At least you have to balance that out by leaving them some worthwhile lessons.

My dad used to say, "You always leave the campground cleaner than when you got there." So you might not have left those cigarette butts there, you might not have left the trash there, but you're gonna pick it up so that the next person who comes gets a cleaner campground. Maybe that's it. Maybe I just want to leave this world better than it was when I got here.

Did I do that, on this particular night? I mean, all we did was shine some light on a building, and in a minute we were going to turn it off and it would be gone. Forever.

Or maybe not.

Maybe what we had put up on that wall was a light that would shine on, long, long after that night was gone.

CHAPTER 6

Jimmy the Back Door Open

After Tempt's light projection, I realized that we'd become part of something I'd been intrigued by for some time.

It's called the Maker movement.

This was still a few years before Chris Anderson, the editor of *Wired,* would write *Makers: The New Industrial Revolution,* the book that became a kind of manifesto for the movement—but its signs were already everywhere.

The Maker movement is sort of an outgrowth of the Hacker movement. The explosion in the number of personal computers in the seventies gave birth to a culture of young people who figured out how to create, in the virtual world, amazing inventions that the big corporations could barely keep up with. They could take apart any program, fiddle with it, make it better, and adapt it to their own uses. To outsiders, they seemed like anarchists; from the inside, they seemed like revolutionaries, people who had taken over the means of production—virtual production—and bent them to their own use.

But now, makers were doing the same thing in the real world. It's one thing to create a new way of buying and selling stocks online, or calculating the growth rate of a business, or a graphical user interface built around the radical concept of Windows, or the million other virtual inventions of the past thirty years; it was another to bring those inventions into the real world.

What we had done with the EyeWriter was the essence of the

Maker movement. We had torn the backs off some inventions in the real world, put them together in a way that solved a particular problem, and posted our solution online so anyone who wanted to could duplicate our results. Makers are all about ignoring the linear way that the business world works: about looking at a problem from a different perspective, figuring out your own solution, and making that solution a reality—not out there in the world of factories and boardrooms and stockholders, but right in the comfort of your own home.

◆

My home seemed ridiculously quiet after the hacker army had packed up and left. One day, about a week later, after we got the kids off to school, Caskey left early to get some work done that she'd put off during the great hackfest, so I found myself alone in the house for the first time in a while. I almost didn't know what to do with myself. I glanced at some headlines on the internet, grabbed a glass of orange juice, and settled in to read the great backlog of emails that had built up.

I never got past the first one, which was from Tempt:

Hi Mick,

I've been having trouble trying to navigate my way around Skype; i'm gonna see if my friend/caregiver Andres can tinker around with it on Monday. He's pretty good with helping me get around my pc, and he's pretty good at figuring out the technical stuff.

The revised drawing program is a bit more difficult to use than the original program. I was discussing this with Evan the other day. It's hard to say how much of it is a result of my bad eyes, and how much is due to the program needing refinement. The original program has more control, but the revised version looks better visually. If only i could control the line better.

I'm still practicing drawing every day, it's a bit better than last Thursday, but not by much. I've saved a couple of the drawings, but i really want to get good at this before showing more stuff, i'm still a lil' embarrassed at how sloppy my stuff is.

BTW, last Thursday was a lot of fun. Even though it took a while to get going, i didn't mind at all. Waiting gave me an excuse to hang with my friends while i drew, which i never get to do these days (i heard they got kinda rowdy outside). I appreciate all the work you and the team have put into this project, i'm eager to watch the developments and be able to be a part of the developments. How are things on your end? Talk soon,

—T

I stared at the words on the screen for a long time, trying to focus on what they were saying, but I couldn't get over the mere fact of their existence.

Tempt was talking to me.

It was the first email I'd received from him. I had sent him my first email a few days earlier, just kind of getting the ball rolling and not knowing what to expect. Now here he was—chatting away like any friend would, talking details about the EyeWriter and the software and whatever.

How cool was that.

We kept emailing over the next few weeks, mostly trying to figure out how to make the drawing program work better for him. His eyes were getting really tired, but he was so dedicated to the task, you could tell it was opening up something in his soul that had been closed off for so long.

As the weeks went on, we continued to make revisions to the system. We now had a whole array of arrows in our quiver—the MyTobii, the EyeWriter, and our painting program (which we were constantly revising). We kept mixing and matching, seeing which

combinations would work best for which activities. We still had a
long way to go with our crude setup, and someone like Tempt, a true
artist, deserves so much more. So we kept trying to figure out how to
make it better, faster, stronger. It was like the hacking weekend had
never stopped; it had just reached a new level.

About two weeks later, Tempt sent another email to me and a
few friends—with a few of the drawings he was working on. I was
blown away.

> Okay, all you b-boys and b-girls out there in kwa-zulu city, check da
> progress . . .
>
> —T Boogie

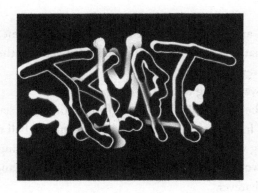

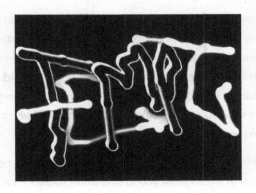

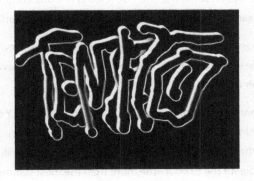

They were still pretty rudimentary—but miles beyond what he'd done that first night. It was thrilling, to see this moving forward so fast.

Those were the last pictures he sent for a while, but we emailed back and forth once a week or so, generally talking details of the program. Tony was really drilling down into what was working and what wasn't. For example:

Hey guys,

i've been messing with the last version of the drawing program (myTAGii), and here are my thoughts:

1) The size of the icons are too large, and they should run along the top left of the window (AWAY from the little icons that minimize, maximize and close the window located at the upper right corner of the screen). Also would be cool to have a wider variety of brushes (like a chisel point), and an icon to select line width. Also, a separate icon to make drips, regardless of which brush you use, or line width.

2) It would also be cool if the drop shadow was an icon, not just a given. That would allow you to stop a line, deselect the shadow effect, then resume the line—so it looks like one continuous line (for example, when you draw the "bar" across a capital "A").

3) Is it possible to have an "underlap/overlap" icon, so you can decide whether or not a line begins underneath a previous line, or over it?

. . . the only other comment i have, is that it's EXTREMELY difficult to control the line with my eyes, as well as ending the line. Even with all the practice i've had since you guys left LA, it's still next to impossible for me to bust little more than the most rudimentary scrawl, which is frustrating because i was hoping to have rocked you some fly styles by now. I'll keep working at it, but so far my tags don't look any different than what you saw when you were here.

Anyway, hope all's well, hit me back anytime, i love hearing what you guys are up to. Stay duggy,

—T

As fall approached, Tempt reported making enormous progress. I was dying to see what he was doing, but he wouldn't show us any more until he was ready.

Then, somewhere in September, he was ready. He sent this email to me and a bunch of his friends:

Enclosed are my first "drawings" in almost 7yrs, done with my eyes in the last 2wks using software created by Graffiti Research Lab, an int'l team of hackers who, like the name says, dig graffiti (Google 'em for more info).

The software is still in development, so it doesn't allow letter connections, but just being able to do some art again is very exciting to say the least. Much respects to TEG and GRL.

I cannot tell you how good it feels to be creative again, and to participate "in the world." This would not have been possible without your friendship and support. Thank you for believing in me. I'm lucky to have friends like you. You are amazing. Your boy,

TEMPTOLEUM

My hands were actually shaking as I clicked on the attachments, and when I opened them up, I nearly fell out of my chair. I yelled for Caskey to come see. They were . . . amazing. They were wonderful.

They were Tempt.

◆

As thrilling as it was, it was still frustrating for all of us. The technology was working, but not as well as it could. We needed to get the EyeWriter and, more important, the software, to where Tempt could use them as easily as you might use, say, a spray can on a wall. We faced a long, meticulous process of tweaking and then tweaking some more.

But we were getting there. And we weren't alone.

I had contacted the folks at Dell, to see if they could help us out, and I'd gotten an incredible, dramatic response: before I knew it I was sitting in a room at Dell with my filmmaker friend Mark Foster and more than a dozen smart people gathered around a conference table. They had done their homework on the EyeWriter—and when I asked, "Is there anything intuitively, that when you look at this thing, you think needs to be changed?"—they all started laughing and talking at once.

So, yeah, they had a lot of ideas. "You're gonna need to see dramatic increases in accuracy, reduction of false positives, all the things that will happen as an evolution over what is now a revolution," said Alex Shows, a Dell engineer. "You're going to see these evolutionary steps to improve the quality of the experience." Geek speak for "we can make this run better"—but still, music to my ears.

See, here's the thing. The inventions we have created at Not Impossible Labs are great. But they are simple. What makes them amazing are the stories that surround these devices. It is the story that makes an invention compelling; it is the story that makes people at Dell jump up and want to help. It's always about the story.

The story is what makes the impossible seem possible. Think of Roger Bannister. For as long as anyone had kept records, nobody had ever broken the four-minute mile. Bannister, a British runner, broke the barrier on May 6, 1954. But his record only lasted forty-six days. On June 21, one of Bannister's rivals broke the record in Finland. We'd gone forever without anyone breaking the four-minute mile, but as soon as one guy did, someone else did, too. I think there's a simple reason: Bannister showed that it was possible. Once something is shown to be possible, the psychological barrier is broken.

That's the power of the story—in this case, of Bannister's story. In our case, it was Tempt's story.

That's why Mark Foster was along for the ride, because it's so important that we document and testify, that we record and relate what we're doing. If you can show, over and over, on a daily basis, that people are doing the undoable, then you diffuse the power of impossible and its hold over people's psyches. You unleash this army of people who are unstoppable, because they think, Oh, I don't have to accept that—I can do this differently. That's what gets really exciting. It's like a video game where you're shooting at a wall: every time someone is exposed to a story of the impossible being possible, it's like one more hit to that wall. Eventually, the wall crumbles and falls, and everyone gets to run through, beyond that wall, into a field of possibilities, and you can say, hey, I want to go play over there. That's a much more fun place to play.

With Tempt's story, we had broken our own four-minute mile—we'd achieved something that seemed impossible. The power of his story—it made people go crazy when they heard it. It enlivened and inspired them.

Which is just what we were after.

◆

Within weeks, the Dell guys had come up with some new prototypes. Drew Tosh, another engineer, brought the best ones out to show to Tempt—including one that sat mostly on top of Tempt's head, instead of on the bridge of his nose, with a tripod that let the camera swivel to follow Tempt's eyes. Tempt stared at Drew intently as Drew put it on himself to demonstrate—it looked kind of like a great big pirate's eye patch—and then we heard Tempt's reaction, through the MyTobii.

"Ha," said Tempt. "Ha . . . Ha."

"He's laughing at you," Caskey explained.

"Is he laughing at the way I look, or the fact that I'm not sure it's going to work right?" said Drew.

Tempt's response, as always, was delivered in the drone-voice of the MyTobii, but was laced with the humor of Tempt himself:

"It's . . . A . . . Pretty . . . Funky . . . Contraption."

The tests were productive, and I was flying so high after that day that I probably just blocked it out when the Dell folks started expressing some concerns over the next few weeks. Their software was based on Tempt being able to double-blink quickly—but after visiting him, they realized that the ALS had progressed to the point where he couldn't quite do that. Dell was also building its version of the EyeWriter based in part on a MyTobii device, which meant, because they were two big companies, they had to work out their own relationship. Unbeknownst to us, those conversations weren't going well. I was thinking, if a roomful of hackers could get this done in a few days, then certainly two of the biggest companies in the field of eye recognition and computing could do wonders if we gave them a few weeks. Which speaks volumes, I think, about the difference between the hacker world and the business world. Because I opened my email late one night and clicked on an email from the project leader at Dell, and it said this:

Mick,

The latest build of the EyeWriter Driver is unable to successfully automate calibration and track the eye as we need it. Furthermore, the efforts underway with Tobii have reached an impasse. . . . I do not believe we will be able to reach a suitable solution for Tony to create art. My sincerest apologies. I had very high hopes and

personal interest in this, and it pains me to know that we have been
unable to improve on the existing software.

Or to summarize the email more succinctly, Dell's out.

I was beyond bummed. But I knew that our "Maker mentality"
got us through the creation of the EyeWriter, and it would get me
through this setback, too. If you can really allow yourself to be part
of that world—to understand that the linear way of doing things has
changed, has metamorphosed—then what used to be a dead end can
suddenly, when you turn it 90 degrees, reveal a new path. It's not
unlike what graffiti did to the art world—busted the boundaries and
the rules and the understanding of what art was, in such a profound
way, that the art community itself had to take notice and pay respect
and finally invite the rebel hordes inside the castle. Such was the way
of the hacker.

The best way to get a bunch of hackers to solve a problem was to
tell them it couldn't be done. And the makers, it seemed to me, were
the next logical step: breaking the backs off things, not in the virtual
world, but in the real world, and taking them apart and putting
them together in a different way. Eventually, I knew, the corporate
world would catch up to us, would understand what we were doing,
and adopt it as their own. So the fact that Dell was not quite ready
to do that yet felt, when you looked at it from that perspective, like
just another step on the path.

I was inspired, and honored, and quite blown away, when Tempt
wrote a little while later, "Things don't always go as planned. But
Mick doesn't give up. If a door shuts in his face, he'll climb through
a window or jimmy the back door open. Ha, ha."

Now, how can you possibly for one millisecond feel sorry for
yourself, when a guy who's paralyzed in a hospital bed and breathing
through a respirator is writing things to try to cheer *you* up? If there
was a moment when I thought of giving up, that blew it right out
of the water.

So the team went to work continuing to refine and play with the EyeWriter and, just as important, the EyeWriter software. And with each fix, it got a little better.

And while we were working on all that, Tempt was working on an idea of his own.

◆

Tempt's friend Angst was the first to hear about it. Angst had been visiting Tempt throughout his long ordeal, but now their visits took on a new purpose. "Once he was able to draw, and once I was back in the rhythm with him of being able to visit and communicate, the subject of our conversations would veer towards art," Angst said. "In these conversations, one of the things I mentioned to him was that I was going to be in a show in Pasadena. He asked about the piece that I was going to have in the show, and I wondered if anyone had approached him to do stuff."

Turns out nobody had—yet. But that didn't stop Tempt. Almost immediately, he went to work on a new piece that he hoped would make it into the show.

And this was no ordinary piece. This was something really, really special.

"He talked about wanting to do something different—that hadn't been done. Not just your paint, graphic, name, inside of a gallery. And when finally the days were getting closer, he said he had a piece he wanted to do."

The piece Tempt had in mind—and, little by little, started committing to paper, through the EyeWriter—was revolutionary in the graffiti world: an attempt to take the flat world of graffiti into the 3-D space.

"I could see each letter going under, over, around, and interlocking with the other letters, like a really complex wild style," Tempt said in an email. But he wasn't talking about painting this. He was talking about making it. In 3-D—actually creating the letters and letting them wrap around each other.

One afternoon, when Angst showed up at the hospital, Tempt showed him a basic sketch.

"Conceptually I thought it was amazing," said Angst. "I knew where it was going to go, as soon as he mentioned it."

When I asked Tempt about it, he wrote, "It came to me in a dream, believe it or not. I had completed a sketch, but to me it's not anything exceptional. It's just your standard graffiti lettering, and for a week after I did it I was racking my brain, trying to think of how to make something different. But everything I thought of was cheesy and lame. But one night, it just came in a dream. Actually. It gave me twelve versions of how to do it. Now, I've got a ton of ideas."

Things started moving fast and furious after that. Tempt hand-picked some famous names in the local graffiti scene to collaborate on the project. He sent a flurry of emails, and there were long visits where he spoke through the MyTobii and moved the project forward. All of his old friends became extensions of Tempt's hands. The project would become a 3-D sculpture of the word *Tempt*, similar to the way he'd get it up on a wall, but with the letters interlocking and bending around each other in complex and unexpected ways. All in front of a background that would be a creative collaboration with the artist friends he'd brought on board.

What was clearly a fascinating new piece of art was rising from our apparent failure with Dell. It made me realize something important about the maker world: Our interaction with Dell wasn't really a failure at all. Not in maker terms. The maker world isn't linear; it's a complex matrix of people and events that are interlinked and interwoven, going in and around and under each other, much like the letters in Tempt's new piece of art. Each person in the process does what they do, and the next person takes it the next step. That's just what was going on in Tempt's world right now: Each of his friends was working on some piece of the graffiti sculpture, or on the background, and none of it was right or wrong. Each was a step that would be modified by the next step, and the next, and the next.

We asked art director Jessie Clarkson to be Tempt's hands. Angst would bring Tempt photos of what they'd done, and Tempt would redirect the efforts: Angle the *M* this way. Tilt the *E* that way. Always striving to get beyond the single plane.

Which, I realized, is exactly what we were doing with the Eye-Writer. Adopting and adapting. Always striving to see it from a different angle. If you use the old business model, where you think in terms of progress and setbacks, you might go crazy and give up. But if you look at it from this new perspective—the perspective of a hive of workers all tinkering with a project in their own individual ways—and if you have the patience and the faith to let that work happen, then eventually they will reach the goal you always wanted to reach but never could have on your own.

I started thinking of the project—and impossible goals in general—in a new way. You have to move from "crowd-sourcing" to something new, something greater—something like "crowd-solving." Not just using the crowd to offer money or ideas, but allowing the crowd to take a stake in the project and push it forward in their own way.

◆

Meanwhile, Tempt was moving the project forward in his own way. He had the kind of visionary approach that I see in my directors: they all have a very clear, creative opinion of how something should be. They know just what they want, and everything around them—language and physicality and computers and cameras and all the rest—become both tools and impediments for them. Because they just want what's in their head to appear on the screen, on the canvas, on the page. Other people and other tools are the membrane through which those ideas must pass in order to exist in the real world. The passion, the purpose, the forcefulness, the clarity with which they will those ideas into the world—I was seeing all that in Tempt, in exactly the same way.

But as clear as Tempt's vision was, the artwork—especially the background mural behind Tempt's sculpture—was becoming even greater than that. It was all the vision of Tempt, but now alloyed with and increased by the energies and creativity and the ideas of his friends. That's exactly what I needed to allow to happen with the EyeWriter. We'd begun with a certain vision, but once we set it free in the Open Source community, other people out there—whoever they might be—would move it forward in ways we couldn't imagine.

Everyone worked together on the mural background, tossing ideas around, goading each other to go a step further and then a step further than that. Some of his friends speculated that maybe that was Tempt's idea all along, to get everyone to come together. The back-and-forth between the fabricators and designers of the giant sculpture took it to places no one had ever gone before in the graffiti world.

Angst had told the folks at the Pasadena Museum of California Art about Tempt's new work, and they were thrilled at the idea of including it, but they weren't sure, at that late stage, if they had the space, given all of the other artists they had already committed to having in the show.

"They got back to us," Angst said, "not guaranteeing anything but saying that it was possible that they would be able to get it into the show. We took that," he continued, with a wry smile, "as a guarantee that it was going to be in the show."

Sometimes, what you believe is what you achieve, and sure enough, Tempt's piece made the cut. The night of the opening, everyone was there—Caskey and me, Tempt's dad, all the graffiti artists—and it was a spooky feeling of déjà vu. It had been more than three years since Caskey and I first went to that art gala that had changed our lives; now here we were again, among the white walls and the white wine and the incredible artwork.

I thought back on that first breakfast I'd had with Tempt's brother and his father, when all they wanted to do was to talk with

Tempt. It took my breath away to see all those people standing and gawking at what Tempt had wrought.

The art that Tempt had created was, finally, able to stand on its own and show itself to the world. It spoke out in a loud and clear and unmistakable voice that Tempt, the artist—not Tempt, the guy in the hospital bed, not Tempt, the guy with the EyeWriter, but Tempt, the artist—had returned.

And what a glorious, glorious return it was.

◆

The sculpture was a testament to Tempt's creative spirit and to his buoyant strength. But I felt like it was a message to me personally, as well. Three years ago, this had seemed impossible. And yet, here it was, huge and proud and impossibly complex and beautiful and, more than anything else, undeniably Here Right Now.

So the only question that remained was: If we had proven, to ourselves if to no one else, that we can make the impossible possible—then what, exactly, do we do next?

CHAPTER 7

The Three Rules of How

"Why did you do it?"

People asked me this question a lot about Tempt and the Eye-Writer. The first time, I was caught off guard. I had never really thought about "why" I did it. I always just focused on the "how" to get it done. So, when I was asked to give talks about the project, I boiled the "how" down to three things.

1. Singularity of focus.

We weren't trying to create the next big thing. We didn't have visions of revolutionizing the medical device industry. We wanted to help Tempt. One person. Had we gone in with visions of sugar-plums and tried to help all people with ALS, we would have missed the mark of creating something that helped Tempt because we would have been distracted. Singularity of focus kept us and keeps us on track.

2. Give it away.

Giving something away is a powerful thing, but I had no idea how powerful it really could be until we did it with Project Eye-Writer. Before we had even created the EyeWriter in the living room of our house, we had decided that it had to be an open-source thing. Understanding the practice of open source within the software world did not prepare me for the effects outside of the world of programming. Without a doubt, the act of giving away the Eye-

Writer was one of the most important and powerful components of the project.

3. Beautiful, limitless naïveté.

Our naïveté was the key to us tackling the EyeWriter with brave abandon. We didn't know that we weren't supposed to be able to do it. We didn't know that kind of thing doesn't really happen in two and a half weeks. We didn't know what we didn't know. And because of that, the entire team just did it because no one ever contemplated or considered the concept of failure.

When the documentary we were making about the EyeWriter project, *Getting Up: The Tempt One Story*, premiered in Park City, a group of computer programmers approached us to tell us how much they had enjoyed the film. It got them talking among themselves about why they thought we had succeeded. Their consensus? "If you had any idea how hard it was to do what you did," they said, "there is no way you would have done it in the first place." They also concluded that they should follow our lead, that they needed to become a little more naïve about what could and couldn't be done. They committed themselves to reevaluating ideas that they had thought were impossible.

◆

So that's what the "how" of the project boiled down to: singularity of focus, giving it away, and beautiful naïveté. But while I was comfortable with my concept of the "how," I was still struggling to answer the "why": Why I pushed so hard to make the EyeWriter for a person I didn't really know at first. Why it was so successful. Why it seems to touch people in such a powerful and meaningful way.

But the more I thought about it, the clearer it became, for me: I did it for my brother, and I did it for my dad, and I did it for my sons.

It's really that simple.

The day I met with Steven and Ron, Tempt's brother and father, it was like looking in a mirror—or, to be more accurate, like looking through a mirror into a parallel world. They were a family just like mine, but different things had happened to them. There's no reason those things couldn't have happened to me. I was just lucky that they didn't. But I could see what the world would have been like if they did.

I am a father. I have sons. I have a brother. I could not imagine what it would be like to not be able to talk to them every day and ask them what they were thinking or feeling. Basic communication was nearly impossible for Tempt. That struck me as wrong.

I don't think anyone who has stared face to face with a reality like that can just walk away and say, "Good luck. I hope everything works out for you." You can't walk away from someone or something that hits that close to home.

And yet, let's face it. Lots of people are faced with terrible realities, and they do walk away. There's nothing morally wrong there; that doesn't make them bad people; it's just a natural part of life. So what was it that flipped that switch in my brain?

When I look for the source of it, for the root of it, I don't have to look much further than my mom and dad.

◆

My father, Leslie Gordon Ebeling Senior, for whom I am named, was a philanthropist, a businessman, and a man who loved spirited debate, though not necessarily in that order. Sometimes, when I was growing up, it seemed like getting us to argue was his favorite activity. This lasted throughout his life: a few years ago, my brother brought his wife's family to meet my dad for the first time. His wife's family is first-generation Mexican from Ensenada, and we're from Arizona, so the immigration issue is a very hot topic on both sides. Before my brother brought the in-laws up to visit, he pulled my dad aside and said, please, let's not talk about immigration at the table, okay? And my dad said okay. And what was the first thing he said when we all got together? Within minutes of the introductions, he asked, "So, what do you guys think about the immigration legislation that's going on?" My brother put his head in his hands, like, are you serious? And my dad was beaming at me, like it was the best opening line he'd ever heard.

But I guess what defined him most was his charity work. My dad and my mom were both involved in charities as far back as I can remember. They started an abused women's clinic in Phoenix together, one of the first ones there. He also sat on the board of Catholic Social Services, and was probably one of the most feared guys there, because, as I said, he loved to start a spirited debate—and if he didn't like your opinion, he wasn't shy about saying so.

But if Dad provided inspiration, my mom provided perspiration: she was the one who was pushy (in a good way), and clear, and saw things through, and wouldn't give up.

One of her biggest achievements, which she worked on with my dad, was called WellCare, which was way ahead of the whole health care debate that's going on today. Here's the problem: A single working mom on welfare gets a guaranteed check and guaranteed health care. If she wants to break out of the welfare cycle, she loses her health care and her check. If she goes to work for McDonald's for minimum wage, she doesn't get health care, and so she might say to herself, "I've got three kids, I can't afford to lose my insurance. The health of my kids is more important to me; I can't afford to go back to work."

So my dad and mom started the WellCare Foundation, a Phoenix-based nonprofit organization that provided free health care from doctors who would volunteer their services so that women could try to break out of welfare. My dad used to call my mom the "trophy collector," because she won so many awards for her work on this.

It's the example my dad set, more than anything he told me, that started me on the path I'm on today. My dad was never much for praising you if you did the right thing—it was understood that you'd do the right thing, so there was no point in making a big deal of it. The fact that he took it for granted made me take it for granted, too. When I told him one day that I wanted to go to college and play basketball—I was not too shabby in high school—his reaction was, "Great. Are you going to shoot baskets every day? How many?" I was startled, and I blurted out, "I'm going to make fifty every day." And sure enough, I started doing that—every morning before school, I'd drag myself out of bed in the room my brother and I shared, slink past the posters of the airborne Phoenix Suns forwards Larry Nance and Darryl "Chocolate Thunder" Dawkins that adorned my walls like a shrine, and head out to the carport.

The basketball hoop was off to the side of the carport. I had helped my dad install the pole into the concrete. The process of learning to mix concrete was a lesson in and of itself, but the feeling of making something for yourself was a feeling that I loved. It was primal. Like killing and eating your food, in a bizarre sort of way.

I'd warm up and then start shooting, and wouldn't stop until I'd sunk fifty, even if it meant being late for school. Usually, as I was nearing the end of my morning ritual, my dad came home from Mass. He went to Mass almost every day at 6:00 a.m. like clockwork. He was the most consistent person I knew. He'd get out of his 1980 Pontiac Grand Le Mans and rebound the final few shots for me before he walked past and into the house for breakfast. I'd gather up my stuff and follow closely behind.

My dad wouldn't make a big deal about my morning ritual. He'd act like, well, of course, that's what you're supposed to be doing. And that, I think, is what motivated me. Those gifts he gave me—the lessons of consistency, of persistence, of assuming that you're going to do what you are supposed to—are the most important gifts I've ever received.

My dad would go off to work while I was grabbing my breakfast. He was always pretty busy with work—first running other companies, then starting his own mortgage business—but he made sure to make time for me and my little brother. As we got older, he would coach my football team—he just wanted to be involved. But one thing that stuck with me was, he pushed me harder than any of the other kids. If they did twenty-five push-ups, I did thirty. If they did thirty sit-ups, I did thirty-five.

I thought it was just him overcompensating, to show that there was no preferential treatment—but I didn't realize at the time that it was, indeed, preferential treatment of the most important kind. Maybe the other kids thought, Wow, Mick's dad is tough on him. And I'm sure there were times that I thought, This really sucks. But when I look back on it, it's one of my fondest memories.

I heard a guy tell an interesting story recently about a meeting of these big, powerful Wall Street guys, where they were all sitting around talking about what deals they'd made, what yachts they'd bought, all that. And this guy had posed a question to them: "What," he asked, "are you guys most afraid of?" It was a conversation stopper. They all got really quiet and thought about it. And one of them finally spoke up and said: "I just want to make my dad proud of me. I'm always afraid of disappointing him." Now, mind you, this guy's dad is dead. And yet he still is motivated by trying to make his dad proud. And it goes around the table, and pretty much everyone agrees.

Wow.

My dad passed away in 2007; I don't think I'm still trying to make him proud—that's not my motivator. I'm not haunted by him, as those millionaires seem to be haunted by their fathers. But I miss him the most when I accomplish something, like creating the EyeWriter and seeing Tempt draw again. I just want to call him up and say, "Hey, Dad, guess what I did today?" He would have been over the moon.

And the difference, I think, is that I am not now, nor was I then, seeking his approval. He exists, for me, as an ethical principle—one that he instilled very, very deep down in me, a place he helped me create within myself that takes pride and pleasure in doing the right thing, and in doing things right. That is the inspiration that drives me, the part that is derived from him.

That's half of what drives me, anyway.

The other half is my sons.

I don't want to be the driving force in their lives, and, frankly, I don't think I could be, should be, or will be. But I do want to be someone they're proud of. I want them to think I take it for granted that you do the right thing. Because, why wouldn't you? I want them to think of that as something as normal as clearing your plate after dinner or doing your homework. Or sinking fifty baskets before you go to school. These are just the things you do, because it's what your dad would expect.

That's how I hope it works, anyway.

We had a pretty nice life growing up in Arizona—we weren't rich by any means, but I didn't want for anything. I got to play sports, we went on great vacations, we went camping in Colorado every year; it was a rich existence.

But when I was a senior in high school, the savings and loan crisis hit. The real estate market went into the toilet, and my dad's mortgage business shrank to almost nothing, because no one was re-financing. It can be pretty scary when your dad pretty much loses his job. I'd see him up in his home office, with an old-school MS-DOS computer and a big floppy disc, churning out letters of application, and I'd see him in the afternoon, getting the mail, opening one rejection letter after another. After a while he was applying for things like manager at a fast-food chain and even getting turned down for that because they were looking for someone younger.

Now, as a dad, I can imagine how incredibly stressful and painful that must have been for him. How embarrassing, how degrading, and how terrifying.

My dad didn't hide his feelings from me. He let me know that these were tough moments for him. But he also showed me something else: that he wasn't going to let this beat him. He didn't stop pushing forward. He didn't give up. He kept doing what needed to be done, for himself, for his pride, for his family. He acted, once again, like this was the most normal process in the world. He had that Winston Churchill worldview—that success is going from failure to failure without losing enthusiasm. Somehow, I knew it would work out, because he made me believe that it would.

I try to pass that lesson on to my sons: that it's okay to get down, to be sad, to be bummed. Those feelings are real. I want my boys to be real when they're sad, and I want them to be real when they're happy. I don't want them to be so immune to pain that they don't have any feelings of sadness. We all know those automaton dads who expect their kids to roll with the punches and stand strong in the face of adversity and all that crap. That sounds to me like the perfect makings of an emotional volcano destined to explode at a later date.

When you feel those feelings of sadness and defeat and loss and pain and disappointment, you allow them in, you sit with them for a while, and then you kick them to the curb and let out a big deep sigh, and get back to doing what needs to be done. You don't throw in the towel. You dust yourself off and get back in the game. I hope my boys have learned that lesson. I hope I've learned it, too.

I learned something important from my mom, as well, during that tough time. She had returned to school, at Arizona State University, to major in religious studies, when the crisis hit. As part of her studies, she was getting credit for working at a hospital as a chaplain, ministering to people of all faiths. But when Dad's business collapsed, she went out and got not one job but two: working as a home health care worker in the daytime, and taking a PM shift at the county hospital's psychiatric unit.

And yet, through all that she never gave up her unpaid work as a chaplain. When I was a kid, I saw how hard she was working, and I think that's where I got the sense that, when tough times hit, you do whatever it takes to keep the family going. But it wasn't until years later that I asked her why, when she was working so many jobs, she kept up her ministerial duties at the hospital. "You were struggling to help the family," I said. "Why would you keep spending time helping others?"

Her answer was quite simple: "I just loved it so much," she said. "It just made me happy."

I wondered where I got that.

Now I know.

◆

In 1988 I went to the Air Force Academy, and that's where I learned my next important lesson. Only it wasn't the lesson they wanted me to learn. What I learned at the Air Force Academy was how to beat the system.

There was a book freshmen had to memorize, called *Contrails*, full of facts and figures that you'd never use in your life, and of course I never bothered to learn it. The book was a hazing ritual for freshmen: the upperclassmen could come up to you at any time and ask you a question out of the book, and you had to answer them. I learned to live with the thrilling fear that any moment I could get caught. It's helpful to get used to that feeling. Comes in handy later on in life.

Anyway, the last month of the semester is called "recognition"— when you're recognized as an upperclassman—and I almost made it through. On the twenty-ninth day, one of the upperclassmen accidentally tripped across the fact that I didn't know anything.

And he pulled me out of my room early in the morning and started screaming at me, in his thick Southern drawl: "Eb-el-LEEN," he called me. Spit was flying out of his mouth, like he was a stark raving pit pull. "Ah don't give a squirt of piss about you. I'm from Tennessee, and you know what we would do to you in Tennessee?"

All of the other freshmen had followed us out into the hallway, because that was part of the process, that your classmates show solidarity. And the cadet starts getting even angrier: "Look at these guys, they have to support you because you're a jackass! You slacker!" And nobody dares to crack a smile, because they know he's already gone batshit crazy and they don't want to make it worse.

"Eb-el-LEEN," he screamed, "Since you don't know anything, we're gonna start with something real simple. We're gonna start with the ABCs, from the top to the bottom." And I started in: "Sir, yes sir! The American alphabet from A to Z is as follows!

"A . . . B . . . C . . ."

And I was going as slowly as I could, and the guy is turning every shade of purple. "Speed it up, Ebeling!" he screamed. And I started going as fast as I could, and then slowing down again. And then I got to the cadence he wanted, and got to "L . . . M . . . N . . . O . . . P . . ." And I just kept repeating the letter, like I couldn't think of what comes next.

"P . . . P . . . P . . ."

"Ebeling! You don't know the alphabet! I can't believe it!"

And the guy next to me, desperately trying to save me, whispered, "Mick, the next letter is Q."

I finally broke character, and with a big grin on my face, stared at the guy who was screaming at me and said, "No shit it's Q."

So now he realizes I've been messing with him. And if you've ever wanted to see what it's like when somebody's head explodes, you should have been there that morning.

Somehow I survived that day. The spirit of being a smartass buoyed me on, but I came to understand that beating the system was way more complicated—and way more fun—than that. I honed my skills as the months wore on. It was all about finding the loopholes and getting through them before anyone knew that you'd found them in the first place.

For example: As a Doolie (which is what they called us as freshman) you were not supposed to make any contact with the outside world, especially during basic training, when you were what they so gently dubbed "lower than whale shit." You were not allowed to make phone calls—and this was 1988, so there were no cell phones or internet, either. So during basic training, I found this weird electrical closet down the hall. It housed two Coke machines and two phone booths. And that was all I needed.

I sneaked in an alarm clock (another thing you were not supposed to have) and set it for three in the morning, when it went off I would hop up and go down to the broom closet. And I would call my girlfriend and my parents in the middle of the night, and talk in whispers. I'd do this three or four times a week, sometimes more. Nothing earth-shattering, just chatting. The point was just to do it, because somebody told me I couldn't.

You see where I'm going with this?

What I learned was how *not* to learn what they wanted me to learn. Look, I understand the whole hazing concept, the whole business of being stripped down to be built back up. It's like this old routine of Bill Cosby's. He says to a guy, "Why do you do cocaine? It's expensive, and, you know, you see all these horror stories." And the guy says, "Cocaine is great. It accentuates your personality." And Bill Cosby says, "Well, what if you're an asshole?"

And that's how I feel about the Air Force Academy. It strips you down to your core, and if your core is weak, they can build you up to what they want you to be. But if your core is strong, and they don't break you, then I think you get stronger. I think I'm the man I am today because of the Academy—but I don't think the Academy would like to admit why that's the case.

It's because I learned to navigate the shark-infested waters. Because I learned that when somebody tells you that you absolutely must do something one way, there's going to be a voice inside you that says, but what if there's another way?

And so I'm grateful for the Academy for what I got out of it.

But I had bigger fish to fry.

CHAPTER 8

There Are Only Monkeys

After the Air Force Academy, I went to UC Santa Barbara, where I began to hone my business skills. In a very college-kid way, of course.

I was following a family tradition: My uncle Gary went to UCSB before me, and helped to start an inter-sorority volleyball tournament. His reasoning was simple: He had a friend who couldn't meet girls to save his skin. His buddies decided to start a volleyball tournament between all the sororities, and told the friend, okay, man, if you can't meet girls running an all-girls volleyball tournament, you might as well hang it up.

When I got to UCSB I fell in with a guy named Seth, who had started this really funky jeans company. He was an artistic guy; he used to draw on jeans with markers, and sell them, and the business did well. So I started going around the college town we lived in and selling them. I would set up these sales events where Seth and I had all these girls try on the jeans and we would "assist" them with the fittings—"Oh, this is a little tight here, let me adjust this for you." (Caskey, who was my girlfriend then, used to come to those sales events and watch us grabbing all those girls' butts as we "helped" them, and just shake her head and laugh at us.)

Pretty soon we put the three ideas together—the sorority volleyball tournament, which was still going strong and had grown to the point where it had become a huge charity event, with half of the Western United States sororities coming; Seth's knowledge of how to make clothing; and my sales ability—and started a company called Deluxe. All those sororities needed matching sweatshirts, tank tops, and shorts for the volleyball tournament, and we were just the guys to sell them to them.

It was a simple concept: I'd drive all around the Western states, going from sorority to sorority with five or six different samples we'd made for less than a hundred bucks, and the girls would come down and try on these tiny, tiny shorts, and I'd take their names and look at their rear ends and take their orders, take their money, and move on. So we had all the money in our pocket before we had to lay out a cent on production. It was a sweet way to put myself through college and a sweet lesson in business as well:

You can make money and still have fun. In fact, it's a lot better that way.

◆

But like most college kids, it was easy come, easy go, and by the time I'd been out of college a few years, the money was spent and I was bored with the job I was doing—selling ski trips and Mexico trips to high school graduates and college kids—and I was looking for a change. Caskey and I had been together for a while at this point, and we were walking on the boardwalk in Manhattan Beach, on the kind of gray January day you don't get too often in Los Angeles but that fit my general mood, and I told her, I want to do something different.

Something very different.

I asked her, "Do you want to move to Spain with me?"

And she let me know she's as tough and single-minded as I am.

"I'm not traveling with you anymore," she said. "I dropped out of art school for you. I moved to Los Angeles. I don't even like Los Angeles. I can't keep my life on hold for you anymore unless you know where this is all going. If we were married, that's one thing, but if we're just fooling around, I'm done."

So I said the only thing a respectable man can say when his back is up against the wall:

"Well, I want to be in Spain by May. If I want you to be in Spain with me by May, when exactly would I have to propose to you by?"

And she kind of shook her head and gave me a funny look, and said, "Okay. Next Wednesday."

She was toying with me. She thought I wouldn't get it together to propose the following Wednesday.

Well, I proposed that following Wednesday.

And two months and twenty-eight days later, we were headed to the airport with one-way tickets to Spain and a total of $1,300 in our pockets.

We threatened ourselves with the following: if we weren't able to figure out how to pay our way over there, we would buy return tickets on credit cards, fly back, and move to a safe, quiet neighborhood, buy a normal car, and get normal jobs, buy a normal house, live a normal life.

Living in fear of the Curse of Normality is a terrific motivator.

We found a cheap hostel to live in. Caskey had sold her car before we left and used the money to buy an old Mac 520c and a little printer, and that was our romantic little honeymoon: printing résumés and looking for a way to make a living.

So we hustled: I went door-to-door in a wool suit in Spain in summer, sweating my butt off. People thought I was nuts: a guy in a suit who doesn't speak Spanish that well, who doesn't even have a visa or work permit—they'd hand me back my résumé, and if my Spanish had been better, I'd have known exactly how stupid they were saying I was.

It got to the point where we were making decisions between buying single sheets of paper from the paper store to print out more résumés and buying a can of potatoes to eat. We didn't want to run up our credit cards because we had no way to pay them off, so we just survived on what we had.

Which was speeding headlong into zero.

But when you have the simple belief that whatever you're told is impossible is what you're going to try—and you're lucky enough to have a beautiful partner who actually believes in that, and in you, and is willing to put up with you on top of it—funny things happen.

So, a funny thing happened. Just when we were ready to fold our hand, we met this guy who ran a school where they taught English. He said, Hey, school is letting out in two weeks—but if you come back in September, I'll give you a job.

Saved!

Now we only had to live until September.

One of our wedding presents was a Eurail pass, and the only phone number we had for anyone that we had even a remote connection to was for my ex-boss's best friend's sister, who was a time-share sales manager at a resort in Portugal, in the Algarve. So we called her, and she said, Oh, God, there's so much work over here! You should come over here and I can totally get you jobs! So we're like, Sweet! It was a waste, really, to cash in that Eurail pass—once you started it, you could travel anywhere throughout Europe for a month, and here we were, about to use it for a single one-way trip—but when you're broke, you're broke, and that Eurail pass was the only way we could get from nowhere to somewhere.

On the train down to the Algarve, we were seated across from a little boy, maybe four years old, playing with some red and blue plastic monkeys. At one point, just to be friendly, I leaned over to him and said, "Hey, those are some cool monkeys you got there. Which ones are the good monkeys and which ones are the bad monkeys?"

He frowned and pulled his little animals close to his chest. "There are no good monkeys or bad monkeys," he said, in that stern voice only four-year-olds can muster. "There are only monkeys."

It became one of those moments—a philosophy lesson served up from a toddler—that stayed with us forever; whenever we got too angry at someone who wasn't helping us reach our goal, through the

Tempt trials and tribulations or many others, and when that anger was only getting in the way, Caskey would turn to me and say, "Remember, there are no good monkeys and there are no bad monkeys. There are only monkeys."

True that.

We got down to the Algarve and phoned our friend. And she said the one thing we couldn't possibly deal with: Sorry, too busy to talk to you today—can we make it tomorrow?

Of course, what we said was, Oh, no problem, we're so excited to have the time to do some sightseeing, it's so lovely here.

And of course, what we were thinking was, How the hell are we gonna survive another day?

Another three days, it turned out: It was three days before she could meet with us, three days during which we would go to the nice hotels and order tea and gobble up the free snacks that came with the tea. We didn't want to walk around too much because we knew we'd get too hungry, so between tea sessions we just sat in our hotel room with our fingers crossed.

Finally, this woman, my ex-boss's best friend's sister, met with us and hooked us up with a guy named Jonathan, who owned a bunch of restaurants in the area. We had put together a proposal for him, where Caskey would do quality control and oversee the waitstaff, and I'd do sales and events with the local hotels, but really we were ready to take anything: We'd tend bar. We'd clean up the bar for the guys who tend bar. We'd mop the floors for the guys who clean the bar.

But Jonathan took a look at my résumé—my last title, at the company that sold the ski trips, was vice president—and looked up at me and said, "Sorry, but I can't afford you."

Caskey slowly and quietly reached under the table and grabbed my knee and dug her nails in. I got the message: You better pull this one out.

So I tried a Hail Mary.

"Look, I know you can't afford to hire us," I said. "But I've looked around at your restaurants, and frankly, you can't afford not to."

Something changed in his demeanor—and although it took a while to seal the deal, I knew we were in. At the end of the day, he hired us; our salaries were small, but to us, they were manna from heaven. After weeks of not eating, we had a free pass at all his restaurants and probably put on ten pounds each in the first week. We had a company car and an expense account for the gas, so we took long weekend trips to Lisbon; on our workdays we'd work about four hours and go for a swim and dine out and toast our good fortune.

We were almost sad when the summer ended, and while we were tempted to not go back and take those jobs at the school, we decided that we should probably continue on our way. So that fall, Caskey was the principal at a school supervising me, this wild six-foot-five guy standing on the desks, teaching "O Captain! My Captain." It wasn't free food and swimming pools, but it was sweet all the same. And I guess, when we tried to weigh the one against the other, we had to say, there are no good monkeys and no bad monkeys, there are only monkeys.

◆

We left Spain that Christmas with round-trip tickets and just a few suitcases, planning to stay in LA just for the holiday and then return to our teaching jobs. But like John Lennon said (and probably a lot of people before him), life is what happens to you when you're busy making other plans.

We got back in touch with Seth, my old college jeans-and-sororities entrepreneur buddy, and he let us sleep on his floor for a couple of days. One morning, one gloriously beautiful California morning that was made for nothing but surfing—which, coincidentally, is what we had planned for the day, and the next day, and the next—Seth woke us up, clacking away at his computer. I asked him, "What are you doing?" and he said, "Oh, it's just this program, it's called After Effects. It lets you animate stuff. I've been doing some freelance work with it." I watched him for a while, and it was pretty fascinating. Kids growing up today are so used to seeing complex digital motion graphics in everything from movies to the news to their own iPad games that it's not in the slightest bit unusual, but in 1996 it was brand-new—nobody I knew had seen anything like the graphics Seth was doing.

I asked him how he made money from the program, and he told me, "People just call me up and ask me to animate stuff."

And I told him in no uncertain terms that that was the stupidest business plan I'd ever heard. Sitting around waiting for the phone to ring. And he asked me, "Well, how would you do it?" And I told him, I'd do what I'd always done, ever since we were in college: I'd go out and make the phone ring.

I started quizzing him and it turned out that there was a big conference in Las Vegas that was about to start called NATPE—the National Association of Television Program Executives—where all of his potential clients were going to be.

We grappled with what was the best course of action—surf or go to the conference. Seth still wanted to go surfing; I wanted to go to NATPE, but I also wanted to go surfing. So we did what any self-respecting UC Santa Barbara grads with surfboards on their minds would do.

We flipped a coin.

Heads, we go surfing. Tails, we go to NATPE.

Seth flipped a quarter in the air, and caught it, and slapped it on the back of his left hand.

Heads. Surfing.

We stared at it for a good three seconds, neither of us saying a word.

And slowly, I reached over, and picked up the quarter, and gently turned it over, and placed it back on Seth's arm.

Tails.

NATPE.

With all due respect to Mr. Lennon: Yes, sometimes life is what happens when you're busy making other plans.

And sometimes, life is what happens when you make it happen.

◆

I hopped on a Southwest flight to Vegas. By night I slummed it in some cheap hotel, and by day I walked from booth to booth at NATPE with an old High-8 clamshell player and said exactly what Seth and some industry magazines I'd studied had told me to say—"Hi, I'm looking for the director of on-air promotions." And I'd find the person and use an old salesman technique—I'd drop the clamshell right at his hands, without saying a word. Something like that is so fragile, your instinct is just to grab it, which is what all of these guys did—and I'd put the headphones on the guy, and hit Play.

And they were blown away. We'd made a video montage from a bunch of pieces Seth had done—maybe 15 percent was client business, the rest just stuff he had done for show—and set it to a killer Beastie Boys track (which is kind of cheating, because everything looks good on top of a Beastie Boys track). And when it was done, they were all pretty impressed.

Then I made the pitch. And this is what took real balls.

After I showed the video to the on-air promo guys, I said, "Well, we would like to be the ones to make your on-air promos, your donuts, and your opens and closes and IDs." And I held my breath, because I didn't know what the hell I was talking about.

But I knew what the hell their answers meant.

Because they all started saying yes.

I came home, and within three months nearly $100,000 in business had come in the door, and with enough good relationships that I took that to something like $1.2 million in business over the next year. Not bad for a business that had done only $100,000 the entire year before, and with a guy who didn't know anything about the TV business making the sales calls. The office was essentially in the store-front basement of our apartment building, the Cricket building, but within a year we had more than a dozen employees. We moved from the Cricket basement to this amazing Frank Gehry–designed office space. Things were hopping.

So let me talk for a minute about business, and balls.

At that point in my life, I was reading a lot of self-help books. I was a sponge for anything that helped you keep a positive attitude. I was listening to Napoleon Hill on tape—he was one of the first guys to talk about the power of positive thinking—and his book, *Think and Grow Rich,* one of the bestselling books of all time. I was listening to Zig Ziglar, and reading *The Richest Man in Babylon*, and what I took away from them was something like what Les Brown used to say all the time: His way of saying it was, Fake it 'til you make it. Mine was: Act like the person you want to be.

People want to know where I come off having this immense confidence, the balls to walk into a room full of professionals and talk the talk when in point of fact I don't know Thing One about their business. But what I took away from all those inspiring books—and more than that, what I took away from my father's lessons on the basketball court, from the business lessons I learned from selling jeans to pretty girls, from getting down to our last penny in Spain— was as profound as it is simple.

You act the way you want to be, and before you know it, you'll be the way you're acting.

Look, everybody walks into a meeting full of fear and self-doubt and thoughts about what-if-I-fail. But think about that for a second. Because the answer to "What will happen if I fail?" is usually simple.

The answer is, usually: Nothing.

Suppose those on-air promo guys had called my bluff. Or dropped the clamshell. Or had seen me for the newbie I was and kicked me out of their booth. Worst-case scenario: they all decided

that Mick Ebeling didn't know jack and they didn't want to do business with me, ever.

So what would I have done?

I would have caught a plane back to LA and gone surfing with
Seth like the coin told us to in the first place. Nothing lost except a
few days in Vegas.

And that's the thing of it.

In those days, every letter I wrote, every email I sent, I signed,
"Take risks, Mick." And that's what people started calling me: Take
Risks Mick. Because the secret to success, for me, was simply realiz-
ing that failure just wasn't that big a deal.

Start with all the mini-risks you take every day. Saying hi to
someone you don't know, speaking up in a meeting when you have a
different opinion from everybody else's, or applying for a job that's a
little over your pay grade. All the petty minor things we think about
and decide not to take a chance on. We get so caught up in what we
should and shouldn't do, and when we translate that for ourselves,
we create meanings around what can and can't be done. These are
not facts—they are conversations that we have in our heads so often
that they solidify and seem like facts to us.

But if you create a different set of thoughts—whether you believe them or not, at first, if you just take another set of thoughts,
positive, motivating thoughts that are just as valid as the fearful ones
you had floating around in your head—then sooner or later (and
most likely sooner) they will solidify as well. And those become the
thoughts that guide your actions, in place of the fearful ones.

And you find yourself going up to perfect strangers and saying,
"We want to make your donuts and IDs," and because you believe
that you can, and more important, because you are acting like you
can, then they believe it as well.

And you have changed reality through the power of what you
say to yourself.

How cool is that.

A study from a couple of years ago found that the average child hears the word "no" more than four hundred times a day—much more often than the word "yes." That "no" can't help but become ingrained in you, so you wind up saying "no" to yourself more often than you can imagine. You walk into situations with the "no" all teed up, ready to go. And when the "no" comes, you were so ready for it, so expecting it, that you accept it for what it is. The final word.

But what if it's not the final word? What if you can retrain your brain to think "yes"—to anticipate and expect the positive, the way you anticipate and expect the negative now? What if you hear that "no" and think, Well, that can't possibly be right, I must have heard incorrectly. That must have been a "yes."

Getting yourself to think differently about life, and the issues you deal with, is called "disruption." Here's another way to look at it: we're taught that the correct order of things is, you put on your underwear, and then your socks, and then your shirt and pants, and then your shoes. Well, what if you put your shoes on first? It would be kind of awkward to get your pants on, and you'd probably have to leave off wearing socks entirely, but what if you did? Or what if you spent a day doing things with your left hand instead of your right—opening doors, brushing your teeth, and so on?

These sound like silly exercises, and maybe they are, but they have profound ramifications. Because nine times out of ten, disrupting the way you usually do things won't get you very far—it'll just get a shoe caught in a pants leg. But one time out of ten, it will show you something completely new and different and fabulous. And if you get yourself in the habit of disrupting yourself, then sooner or later you're going to trip across that fabulous disruption.

And the most important thoughts to disrupt are those thoughts of failure—those fears about what might happen if you make a fool of yourself. Because those are the ones that get you stuck in the ruts you can't get out of.

Here's another example. We all grew up driving with our hands at 10 and 2 on the steering wheel. Turns out that's not safe, in the age of airbags. It's safer to keep your hands at 9 and 3. We all grew up adjusting our rearview mirrors so that you could see the tail of your car. Turns out, that creates blind spots that go away if you turn the mirrors a bit farther out so you can't see the tail of your car at all.

After learning the old way, the first time you get in your car and put your hands at 9 and 3, and tilt the mirrors so you can't see your car, you feel really weird and exposed. Doesn't matter that someone tells you it's better or safer. It's just different from what you know, and you have to take it on faith that it's right, even if it feels strange.

Same with imagining a "yes" when you're expecting a "no"—or acting confident when you're feeling nervous.

You just fake it 'til you make it. Act like the person you want to be.

◆

Seth named his company Fuel, and it was taking off like a rocket ship. But even though the business was hopping, and I was the one who was bringing it in, it still seemed kind of unreal to me. I mean, Seth was paying people well—we had designers who were making $500 a day —and I kept stopping in my tracks, and looking around, and thinking, this is crazy! This is silly money! People are getting $500 a day for sitting at a computer and moving things around on a screen?

And it occurred to me—what if you actually told kids about this? That you could play around on a computer all day, doing silly stuff, and make a ton of money doing it? What if we let kids in on the fact that such a thing was even possible?

What would happen if they knew?

Caskey and I started talking about it, and we decided early on, let's not go into the fancy suburbs like Brentwood where all the moms and dads are creative directors and designers and editors. Let's go into the inner-city schools and say, hey, did you know there's a profession called animation? A profession called art direction? Jobs called rigging and modeling and texturing and lighting? And it all happens on a computer—and you like to mess around on computers anyway?

And so that's what we did. We started a little side program called Digital Groove. We got into high schools—Hollywood High at first, and then we expanded to Venice High—and Caskey built a curriculum for the kids that covered all the bases.

The program began with the kids coming up with a project, and at the end they delivered a film. We got all their teachers involved: as the kids went through the program, they had to write a script—that was done in English class. And they had to present storyboards— that was art class. They had to do their research—that was social studies. The projects had to be related to whatever was going on in their history class; so for example, one group of students who were studying the 1920s did a project comparing speakeasies to raves, and modern-day gangbangers to Prohibition-era gangsters. And of course they had to do the animation, which was computer science.

So the whole core curriculum was wrapped up in project-based learning, and at the center of it was teaching kids this brand-new digital technology and lots of other aspects of filmmaking. They had to meet with us two nights a week for three hours a night, and we had dozens of volunteers, from all over Hollywood, working with them. We had people who'd worked on *Jurassic Park* showing them how to make a baby dinosaur coming out of an egg; we had makeup artists teaching them how to make scars.

It was fabulous—the kids were passionate about it. Attendance went up. In our group, there were no arrests, no teen pregnancies, none of that. I don't want to go too far in taking credit for any of that—it was a small sample, so it was hard to judge. But it was pretty clear that engaging kids in something they were passionate about gave them something to do other than get into trouble. More important, it gave them a chance to feel good about themselves and to believe that they had a future worth thinking about, and I saw firsthand how life-changing that can be. When the kids started the program, we asked them what they thought they'd be doing after high school, and the surveys came back: Janitor. Burger flipper. Gardener. Retail sales. At the end of the year, we took the survey again, and the answers came back: I want to be an editor. A writer. A director. And, of course, a digital artist.

The kids were responsible for going to all their classes during the day and doing their homework, and then showing up for our sessions. And the mentors would read them the riot act if they showed up without their homework or without having their program work done.

I remember very clearly one of our volunteers looking a kid who was slacking off straight in the eye and saying, "Do you know how much money I make? Do you know I have to beg my boss to get time off to come work with your sad ass, so I can teach you things so you can make as much money as I make? Don't waste my time. I'm not getting paid for this, and I'm not showing up to babysit you, so if you don't want to do the work, I'll just tell Mick to kick your sorry ass out of the program. Welcome to the real world, kid."

The kid was flabbergasted. I don't think anyone ever talked to him like that. But he showed up with his act together the next week, that's for sure.

◆

When I think about Digital Groove, and all that came after it, I think about an old woman and her groceries.

Imagine you're sitting in a Starbucks, and this little old woman is carrying her groceries across the street, and she trips and falls, and her groceries go everywhere. And you look out of the corner of your eye, and you see a car coming. It's down a ways, but it's coming. What do you do? Do you sit and finish your coffee? Do you say, Oh man, it's the perfect temperature right now, I need a lid and some sugar cubes? Or do you hop up and go help the old lady?

That's kind of how I felt with Tempt and the EyeWriter. When I met a young man who said to me, "I just want to talk to my brother again," well, I'm a brother, and I can relate to that. When a father says, "I haven't talked to my son in seven, eight years," well, I'm a father, and I can relate to that. So when you think of the old lady and the groceries, you realize that, in these moments, it's all about just getting up out of your seat.

Years later, I wound up giving a TED Talk about all the projects we were working on, and it boiled down to that simple phrase: "If not now, then when? If not me, then who?"

It became a mantra that I lived my life by, the idea that gave birth to all the other ideas.

It was the same with Digital Groove; I was, like, wait a second, so these people are making $400, $500, $600 a day, and there's only white people here? And they're all people who had opportunity? Let's get up out of our comfy chairs and put down our coffee and give this to someone who needs it. Someone who doesn't have the opportunity.

And once you do that, once you get out of your chair and realize that by a simple action you can create an enormous change—I don't mean to overstate it, but you see a shift in the community, and you see these kids start to make money and take it back to their neighborhoods, and that's where they're spending their money. That's how you can create real societal shifts.

And you realize, this is addictive.

Screw the coffee.

◆

I left Fuel after a year or so and started out on my own, freelancing at first. I did some executive producing, increasing my knowledge and my contacts until I was ready to start my first company. It was called They. I started it in 2001 with Caskey and a friend, and it was an extension of what I'd been learning at Fuel and in the time since—how to bring digital concepts to different markets. We had some pretty cool clients: NASA, among others. That was a great scene—all these G-men in gray suits and ties, and me, this crazy guy from LA with bleached white hair, extolling the virtues of all we were going to create for them. And they totally got it. And so did a lot of others.

But when 9/11 happened, the bottom fell out of our business—nobody seemed to want to spend money on anything for a while—so Caskey threw us a going-out-of-business party worthy of the *Titanic* (but instead of a violin quartet playing while everyone drank champagne, it was Outkast and Lenny Kravitz blaring on the stereo while people drank vodka being poured down a twenty-foot ice luge).

I kicked around freelancing and consulting for a few years until the economy started to pick back up. We started The Ebeling Group, and things started clicking. Even before we got the *Stranger Than Fiction* and *Quantum of Solace* gigs, I knew we had created something special.

But I don't think I knew how much the experience with Digital Groove had affected me—the idea of giving yourself joy by giving something away, not money, but time and effort and commitment, in a way that was meaningful to someone who truly needed help. Certainly, the experience I had with Tempt was the culmination of that.

Or it seemed like the culmination, anyway.

Little did I know it was just the beginning.

CHAPTER 9

Tapping the Passion
of the Personal

Parents who've sent their grown children out into the world tell me it's both thrilling and terrifying: You have kept them in your sight for so long you can't imagine them surviving without your tender loving care; yet you know you've prepared them for that moment, and you can't wait to find out the places they'll go and the people they'll meet.

I kind of had that feeling when they sent the EyeWriter out into the world. Once you give up your baby to open source, you never know what's going to happen.

But we were about to find out.

One day, we got this email:

From: Kyunghwa Yu
Date: Tue, Dec 13, 2011 at 5:33 AM
Subject: The eyeCan project

Dear who may it concerns.

This is Kyunghwa Yu from SAMSUNG C.Lab.

We are so happy to tell you that we're developing eyeCan inspired by your eyeWriter.

113

eyeCan project is

—developing software

—for people who cannot move their bodies for Lou Gehrig's disease or Lock In Syndrome

—to allow them to access computers and connect with the world (by themselves and without the help of others)

It is based on open source design from eyeWriter but we modified software to use computer and added more functions such as exploring google street view. And we will also provide DIY kit to people in need in south Korea.

So I just want to tell you that thank you for your idea, eyeWriter. It inspires us and let us to help people in need.

◆

It had been two years since our adventures with Tempt. Two years since we'd sent our little child out into the world. I got a huge thrill, a wave of excitement and happiness, when I got that email. It's a perfect example of what can happen when you open-source your world.

We had hoped that some little gang of crazy hacksters somewhere would do what we did with the EyeWriter—look at it, play with it, improve it, find people who needed it, give it away. We just never imagined that the little gang of crazy hacksters would be part of one of the biggest technology companies in the world.

But that's just what happened. A small group of engineers at Samsung Electronics, as a fun little project on the side of their main work, had adopted, adapted, and improved our design for the EyeWriter. The result, which they called the eyeCan, was just as open-sourced as our own: Samsung didn't produce the eyeCan for sale. They provided the software, they uploaded the instructions on how to make it, and anyone who wanted one could build it for about fifty bucks.

They entered into an agreement with the government of South Korea, which agreed to build the eyeCans and distribute them to patients who needed them. I read one report that it was going to more than two hundred patients that year, and that the Samsung engineers were figuring out how to "export" their private-public partnership concept to other countries.

So when you think of a computer virus, you think of some kind of malware. And when you think of something going viral on the internet, it's usually something dumb like a selfie video of someone crying about Britney Spears, or a guy getting hit in the balls with a baseball bat, or something like that.

But think about this. Think about Tempt, a lone, solitary figure in a hospital room. Think of the sound of that respirator he listens to, all day, every day. Think about his art and how that art reached out to the world in an art gallery on a night when I happened to be present. And think about how much has occurred because of his art, that benefit, that night: How it led to hooking up with those crazy guys with their laser painting and to all those other hackers, and how it reached all the way to some engineers at Samsung, and to the government of South Korea, and beyond. And it reached into the solitary hospital rooms of hundreds of other ALS patients all around the world, sitting and listening to their respirators, all day, every day, only wishing they could communicate with their brothers, their sisters, their mothers and fathers. And now they can.

Can you doubt—even for one second—the power of giving things away, the power of making things accessible, and the incredible force that's unleashed when you truly believe that nothing is impossible?

And that was only the start of it.

Because once I had a taste of how far you can go when you make things free and accessible, I was hooked.

I had experienced what it felt like to create something that everyone said was impossible, for someone who really needed it. And all I wanted was to have that feeling again, and again, and again.

And that's what we were doing while our little child, the Eye-Writer, was out wandering the world. We were forming, and building, and gestating an idea that we were now ready to spring on the world.

That idea was what we called the Not Impossible Foundation.

Not Impossible was a way for Caskey and me to find others like Tempt who needed help, and find a way to match them up with people like our hacker team who could figure out simple, cheap solutions for them.

I'm a producer, so one of my first thoughts was also to make this idea of matching people with solutions into a TV show. Caskey and I, along with an employee who'd been with us the longest, Summer Breault, started brainstorming what that show might look like. Every week, our mission would be to solve a critical need by hacking or making something. We had a great name for the show, too: *Making Good*.

We put together what they call in the TV business a "sizzle reel"—a kind of demo of what the show would be like, based mostly on the footage of the EyeWriter that Caskey had shot for the Tempt documentary—and we started shopping it around to networks. The initial reaction was insane: buzz like you wouldn't believe. Everybody loved the idea. They were excited about the story of Tempt. And then they asked, so, what would your other episodes look like?

And we started to describe some of our other ideas.

And they were a little less than excited.

And we described a few more.

And they were even less excited.

It felt like the room had sprung a leak and all the air was draining out, and all the enthusiasm was draining out along with it.

Now I don't want you for a second to think that this was a failure of creativity: far from it. Caskey and I had surrounded ourselves with some amazingly creative people, and we'd come up with some great ideas for episodes.

But there was definitely something missing.

What made the Tempt project successful, as I've said, were three things: singularity of purpose, open source, and a beautiful naïveté. This TV project was centered on all of those. But it was still missing a key component. Because there was a fourth element in the Tempt project that infused the other three with electricity and drive, that kept people up until four in the morning solving the riddles, annoying glitches, and big theoretical problems, all at once.

That fourth element was the passion that comes from a personal connection to whatever needed to be solved.

From the moment I met Tempt's family, I was filled with passion around their plight. How could you meet these people, feel their pain, and possibly say no to them? Throughout the build, we encountered so many roadblocks that we had to go over, or under, or around. Or sometimes, blow them up entirely. Sometimes we needed finesse to keep the EyeWriter project going. Sometimes we needed dynamite.

That passion was our dynamite.

In our TV pitch for *Making Good,* we had come up with a lot of interesting ideas for episodes—but we had not come up with that core, visceral motivating factor. We had not come up with the passionate personal connection. That was the passion we needed to make the other projects work.

And in a simple moment that changed our lives forever, we realized something very humbling.

We could not do this on our own.

So we invited the whole world to help.

◆

Our idea was simple: create a website where people can write in with their impossible problems, problems like Tempt had. My son wants to draw again, but he's paralyzed. Impossible.

Then we would open the question up to the world, and see if someone can come up with a way to make it NOT impossible.

And then, we go build it.

It took a while, but in the spring of 2011, we were up and running. We started test-driving the concept around to investors, and from the first meeting, we knew we were tapping into something. And from the get-go, we started hearing about unsolvable problems—and started to find astounding solutions.

The TV show idea got put on hold.

The let's-go-out-and-do-these-impossible-things idea took over.

One of the first emails that came to us was from a guy named Chuck, who contacted us about his son, Alex, who is nineteen years old and paralyzed from the neck down. Chuck was looking for a way to make it possible for Alex to continue his education online and through interactive media.

Alex could use an eye cursor similar to what we'd created for Tempt—a device that allowed him to control the cursor on a laptop with his eye movements. But it was impossible for Alex to watch a lesson online—much less participate in it—while using the eye cursor. Imagine if you had to take notes with your eyes, while trying to watch and listen to something else. Impossible, of course.

And then.

I ran into James Powderly, the genius from GRL who helped mastermind the EyeWriter. We got to talking, and he said, Hey, Mick, is there anything else I can do for you guys? And I said, Funny you should mention. Wanna join a team?

And just like that, we were off to the races.

Chuck was hoping we could come up with a "mouth mouse"—similar to those devices that allow quadriplegics to operate a wheelchair by blowing into a tube. The "mouth mouse" that was available ran upwards of $800. James and some of his Korean friends and coworkers started looking at how to make one that was as good as what was out there, but for a fraction of the cost.

A company in Colorado called Sparkfun and some guys at the advertising agency Team One picked up the ball. Sparkfun is an electronics firm that sells parts for prototyping, and that's dedicated to making industries think a little differently—right up our alley. They think they can help us make a "sip-and-puff" mouse for between thirty and fifty bucks. We're calling it the Alex Mouse project.

The projects that were starting to pop up for us all had those key components we had isolated in the Tempt experience. One, there was a singularity of focus. If I say, let's go out and try to cure malaria, or let's see if we can find a solution to hunger in America, it's too overwhelming. You lose your way, like trying to take a hike in a blizzard at night. But if I say, Jimmy has malaria, Jane is hungry. Can you help those two people? Then the problem becomes something you can attack without losing your mind. There are people trying to solve the problems of malaria and hunger, and God bless them. Better men and women than I. But for me and our group, this concept—the singularity of focus as a starting point for solving a problem—became key. Our motto became: help one, help many.

Second, Alex Mouse was open-source. Because no one was trying to "own" the Alex Mouse, we were able to get a whole bunch of people involved in conceptualizing the problem. In fact, multiple teams have jumped on the project.

Third, there was that beautiful naïveté. Just as with the Eye-Writer, we didn't have any idea of how likely it was that we might or might not succeed.

And fourth, we had the passion that comes from personal connection. You simply could not talk to Chuck, Alex's dad, and not be infected with the burning desire to make the Alex Mouse project happen. When a father is saying to you, please, my son is paralyzed, and he wants to go to college, can you help me—you have no choice. Right now—try saying "no" to that father, out loud. You can't. You have to help that father. And that son.

And that is what is at the center of it all. At the center of it all was Alex, a boy with a simple but profound need. And all the people who became involved in the project were inspired to passion by that single need.

So the question for all of us is, who is your Alex?

The team on the Alex Mouse was off and running. They had their cause that they were unable to say no to. We're still working on it, but as a friend of mine likes to quote, from the old Billie Holiday song: The difficult, I'll do right now; the impossible will take a little while. So I'm hoping the spirit of Billie will carry this one to completion. But the question remained: Which would be the next project I would be unable to say no to?

Who would be my next Alex, my next Tempt?

I was about to find out.

◆

The EyeWriter opened a lot of doors for me. Suddenly, I could call people up who probably wouldn't have taken my calls before. I mean, I have a very successful production company, and the phone rings and business comes in, but at the end of the day I still have to make it ring, and we're competing with a lot of other folks for a finite number of jobs. But now all of a sudden I was playing in this brand-new space—a space that had nothing to do with advertising or film or TV or anything else—and fascinating people were reaching out to ask me about it and to tell me about other people who are doing some pretty impossible things.

Ever since we started the Tempt project, I had poured a good majority of the profits of The Ebeling Group into what would become Not Impossible. I know I was putting the company and my family at a little bit of a risk, but I was just like my mom, with her chaplaincy: I was so damned happy doing what we were doing that I just couldn't stop.

Caskey and I realized, though, that we were at a point where we wanted to grow Not Impossible into something that wasn't entirely dependent on The Ebeling Group, and to do so we would have to bring on people who had the ability to play big—while still understanding what it means to be a start-up.

More important, I didn't want to be susceptible to the whims and trends of corporate giving. We needed to be self-sustaining if we were going to keep helping one and helping many. And so the foundation gave birth to Not Impossible Labs, a for-profit arm of the same concept. In the year or so that followed, there rose up a volcano of interest around us—Not Impossible Labs just had a magnetism about it, attracting brilliant people who were like-minded, passionate, and who wanted to get involved in some way.

One of those people was Elliot Kotek.

I met Elliot at a dinner thrown by a mutual friend, Will Travis. Elliot has a science and law background, and also happened to be running a number of magazines. When I met him, he'd been doing a lot of bio-tech venture capital, including work that was around what's called an "innovation investment fund," which helped banks invest in really good scientific ideas. So he had a background in finding funding for ideas that help people and a background in storytelling.

Elliot was familiar with Caskey's documentary on Tempt, since he had been the editor in chief of *Moving Pictures* magazine, where he had covered Sundance and Slamdance every year. He'd also previously interviewed Caskey for the magazine, about a short film she'd done called *The Package*.

I was talking with Intel at the time; they were interested in finding good stories out there that they could get behind and maybe create some branded content for their website. Elliot started working for us on finding short films and documentaries out there that might fit the bill for Intel. He worked a couple of blocks away from us, so he'd pop in on us pretty often to toss around concepts. The more I hung with this guy, the more I loved how sharp he was, how much he loved bad puns—and the more I came to know that he was destined for a bigger role with us than he was envisioning for himself.

One night when Caskey and the kids were out of town, Elliot and I went out to dinner at a nice fish place that had opened on Abbot Kinney in Venice. I said, "You know, I need a guy who has a law background," and he started suggesting some people. And I said, "You know, I need a guy with a law background and also a medical background," and he started suggesting some people. And I told him, "You know, I need a guy who has a law background, and a medical background, and maybe he's run some magazines . . ." And finally he got the point and started to laugh.

"Look," I told him, "I'm going to make you an offer. I'll write it down on this napkin."

I slid the napkin across the table to him.

It was blank, of course. I mean, I didn't have the money to pay anyone. So it was the best offer I could make.

Turned out, it was an offer he couldn't refuse.

"So, how about it?" I said. "Do you want to try to do this thing with me?"

And he said, "Sure."

And I said, "Cool."

And he had his fish, and I had a steak, and the next chapter of Not Impossible began.

I can't overstate how important it is to surround yourself with the right people. I had the passion and the drive to propel Not Impossible into existence—but to help take it to the next level, I wanted an Elliot. Even though I wasn't paying him, he was working in our offices more and more—while still holding down his paid jobs elsewhere—and before I knew it, he had hired our first staff member (while I was on vacation, mind you), brought in his friends to redesign our logos and overall look, and we continued to grow around my core Not Impossible philosophy.

After we'd created our website for people to write in with their impossible problems, we decided the site should also highlight all the great works that were going on in the world—all the other Not Impossible projects out there. We had started running Not Impossible stories on our website a while back, about some of those amazing people. One of the first stories—and, as it would turn out, one of the most serendipitous—was the tale of Richard Van As, a carpenter who lost four fingers in a circular saw accident and who had the darkest sense of humor of anyone we'd come across. "After my accident, I was in pain, but wouldn't take painkillers. I barely slept, and the more pain I had the more ideas I got," he said. "Sometimes you have to chop fingers off to start thinking." What he started thinking about was how to make a mechanical hand that didn't cost the $10,000 that the current state-of-the-market hands cost; once he made one for himself for under $500 bucks, he started making them for other amputees, too. He dubbed his remarkable homemade device the Robohand.

We also heard from Nicholas Negroponte, the founder of the MIT Media Lab and the guy who helped start the magazine *Wired*. Nicholas had started a wonderful operation called One Laptop per Child, which was spreading internet access across underdeveloped nations. In November of 2007, he launched a program called "buy one, give one"—if you bought a laptop for your kid, One Laptop would donate one to a child in a developing nation. It was absolutely mind-blowing, the ramifications of that. My production company had produced a commercial for OLPC, so I had some familiarity with their operation.

One of Nicholas's initial mantras was "move bits, not atoms"—in other words, operate in the virtual world the way we used to operate in the real world. The whole mantra of the new Maker movement is just the opposite of that—do with atoms what we've been doing with bits for the last ten years. Do for the real world what hackers have done to the virtual world: disrupt it, turn it around, and make it work in a whole new way.

Nicholas is one of those people who loves to connect other people to each other, like I do, and he introduced me to a guy named Matt Keller. Matt used to be with OLPC and now was working at the X Prize, another incredible group. The X Prize team sets goals that have the potential to help humanity in one way or another—life sciences, sustainable energy development, and so on—and then gives a big cash award to the first person to achieve that goal. So rather than giving awards to great achievements, they put the money out there as an incentive to achieve greatness. Brilliant. And not coincidentally, one of their catchphrases is "making the impossible possible."

Matt is incredibly focused and passionate about serving others. Just to give you a sense: He wanted to become a Jesuit priest, so he thought of enrolling in a Jesuit monastery. But when he realized that the priesthood wasn't for him, he joined the Jesuit volunteer corps instead, to continue to be "a man for others" (the fundamental Jesuit concept) as a volunteer. He was passionate about the cause of homelessness, and that passion took him to Washington to work for Senator Dale Bumpers. His passion then took him to Arizona to do battle on housing issues for migrant farmworkers. Once he realized that the real problems stemmed from the corrosive effect of money on politics, he returned to Washington to work for Common Cause on the issue of campaign financing, working closely with Senator John McCain's office for several years. After that, he joined the United Nations' world food program, to lobby governments around the world on issues affecting poor schoolchildren.

What impressed me about Matt was that he continues to drill down into what he wants to change, and he doesn't stop until he gets to the root.

Truly, a man for others.

I met Matt at a restaurant just down the street from me, and over dinner he told me he was working on the X Prize for Global Literacy. He told me about another amazing person he'd heard about: Dr. Tom Catena, a lone physician working at a remote hospital in the mountains of Sudan, to help people who were injured in the ongoing civil war.

"A lot of the people injured are kids who have lost arms," Matt said.

Something clicked. I flashed on Richard Van As and his Robo-hand, and on the feeling of just taking the leap of faith, and I heard these words coming out of my mouth:

"Well, we should just go make hands for them, then."

Matt was silent, for a moment. So was I.

"What do you mean, we should go make hands for them?" Matt finally said.

"We should just go do it." I didn't know how else to say it—and I didn't realize that "we should just go do it" would become another little mantra for our company.

Suddenly, Matt was very checked in. I explained that we could use a 3-D printer to make the kind of mechanical arms that Richard Van As had made; we could haul the printers over to Sudan—like I was even aware of what it would mean, to go to Sudan, let alone try to haul in a couple hundred pounds of gear—and make them right on the spot.

"How long would something like that take?" Matt said, hesitantly.

"I mean, if you could arrange the visas for me, I could be over there next Wednesday. I could do it sooner, but my kids have a soccer game this weekend," I said, kind of flippantly.

And so it began.

We each ordered another glass of wine and I started brainstorming about how we might actually do this. But toward the end of the conversation, I sensed that Matt thought I might just be blowing hot air.

So I told him: "Don't challenge me to do something like this. Because if you say let's do it, I'm in."

All in.

When I went home that night after dinner, everybody was asleep. The house was quiet, but I was inspired and full of energy. When I come home late, I usually just go around and shut off the lights, grab a glass of water, and head upstairs to bed. But on this night, I sat down in the now dark kitchen, opened up my computer, and Googled Dr. Catena. I spelled his name wrong a few times, but eventually I saw in the search queue an article in *Time* by Alex Perry, dated April 25, 2012, under the headline "Alone and Forgotten, One American Doctor Saves Lives in Sudan's Nuba Mountains."

It was all I needed to see.

The article was written at the Mother of Mercy Hospital, deep in rebel-held territory in southern Sudan's Nuba Mountains. In it, a fourteen-year-old boy named Daniel Omar describes how, on a bright clear day in early March, a bomb dropped by his own government blew off both his hands.

"I was at El Dar, taking care of our cows," Daniel says in the article. "I heard the sound of an Antonov so I lay down. Then I could hear that it had released a bomb and it was coming down on me. So I jumped up, ran behind a tree, and wrapped my arms around it."

The tree saved Daniel's life, but the explosion ripped his hands off.

"I saw blood," says Daniel. "I saw my hands were not there. I could not even cry. I stood up, and started walking, then I fell down. A soldier came and picked me up and put me in the shade. Then he got a car. And they washed and bandaged me, and brought me here."

The article went on to talk about Dr. Catena, how he refused to pull out even when his overseers excavated the region and told him to leave, how he stayed and did amazing work in caring for boys like Daniel. All I could think was, as a father, what if that happened to one of my boys?

From the kitchen table where I was sitting, I could see down the hallway to where my three boys were sleeping. I got up and walked to their room and peered in, and I thought: What if Daniel were my son?

And in a sense, in that moment, he became just that.

Because now the idea had a singularity of focus.

I could not stop the war in Sudan. I could not end bloodshed and slaughter and the maiming of innocents.

But I could help one boy.

I could help Daniel.

◆

Matt and I talked, again, several times, over the next few days, and the ball began rolling pretty fast.

I did the same thing I'd done with the Tempt project. Commit first. Then figure it out later.

I got in contact with Richard Van As, and told him my plan, and he couldn't have been nicer—well, let me correct that; he is one of those people who seems grumpy at first, but through that veneer of grumpiness, he is about as responsive as he can be, and he promised to help any way he could.

A few days later, I was driving to Santa Clarita in our electric car when the battery died, so I had to sit in a café while it charged, which was perfect—stuck with my computer in the middle of nowhere for a couple of hours, I wrote the complete sponsor proposal, then and there. It was what we call a deck, which is basically a PowerPoint for investors explaining what we need the money for.

A week later I took a meeting with a friend of mine who was a creative director at Intel, and she was psyched about the idea. She immediately pitched it to her bosses, who immediately jumped on board: they were going to give us computers, and support, and money to help pay for the trip.

Not a bad start.

That same week, another fortuitous connection fell out of the sky, in the form of a guy named Oliver Laubscher.

My first meeting with Ollie was very unusual. He was the head of business development for GroupM, a division of WPP, the world's largest media holding company. I was introduced to him by a mutual friend and colleague, Paul Lavoie. I was meeting with Ollie about the *Not Impossible* TV show when he stopped me and said, "I hate to interrupt, but I have to tell you I've followed you for a while. I know all about Tempt and the EyeWriter. I've actually built my own EyeWriter." Now, outside my circle, I had never met anyone who had built their own EyeWriter "just because," so we bonded instantly. While GroupM didn't get involved with the TV show, Ollie and I stayed in touch. Even as I was starting to conceive how to build arms for Daniel, Ollie and his boss, Peter (another amazing guy), were having conversations with us about how to get more deeply involved with Not Impossible.

What I didn't know was that Ollie had a second life running marketing for a family business called Precipart, a global company with facilities in Switzerland, the UK, India, and the United States. Precipart provides precision mechanical components—gears, motion control systems—to industrial aerospace customers in more than thirty countries. They also specialize in medical devices. The perfect company for this project. They are one of those large multinational companies you might live your entire life not knowing about but what they do could very well affect you on a weekly basis. The next time you land safely in a Boeing 747, it's probably because of the something intricate and precise that Precipart helped make.

◆

It was September now, and even though Intel had offered support, you never put all your eggs in one basket, so I was beating the bushes, trying to find more sponsors to help pay for Project Daniel. I had just finished up a meeting at the GroupM offices in Santa Monica—Peter and I met in person, and Ollie was on the speakerphone—and was driving back when my phone rang. I pulled over and answered it. It was Ollie. I assumed he wanted to talk more about the phone call we'd just wrapped up less than thirty minutes earlier.

"Hey, man, can I talk to you?" he said. "I'm not talking to you as a GroupM person. I'm talking to you on behalf of Precipart, my family's company."

Well, it's a good thing I had pulled over, because when I heard what he wanted to tell me, had I been driving I certainly would have run into something. He said his family had just had a company retreat. They had watched my EyeWriter TED Talk, and they said, "We gotta get involved with what Mick is up to." And what better way to get involved than to be a sponsor of Project Daniel?

I was beyond stoked, because I couldn't think of a better partner than a multinational company that made practical touch-it-with-your-hands technology. I told him how happy and honored I was and that we would continue to talk to sort out all the details and the timing of their involvement.

Now keep in mind, I still didn't have the slightest idea of how to 3-D print an arm for Daniel. But hey, you can't get stuck on the details.

People had started coming forward to help us with the logistics, with the mechanics, with the publicity. There was one group in Rhode Island and one in Kansas City, each printing parts of Richard's Robohands and shipping them to us in Venice, just as a backup—so that if we got all the way over there, and the printers weren't working, we'd have spare parts to make hands from. Our main priority was to do everything "in country"—but we wanted to have a contingency plan, just in case. Intel was on board and was providing the tablets we would use among other things, and Precipart had scheduled a meeting for me to meet with their executive team three weeks before I left for Africa.

One of the coolest guys who jumped on board was Brook Drumm, the founder of a 3-D printing company called Printrbot. At this point I still didn't know anything about 3-D printing. We started calling around and were just not getting any love from 3-D printing companies; no one really wanted to partner with us.

Which honestly surprised the heck out of me, since I figured that this would definitely be something that a 3-D printing company would jump on.

Every company was willing to sell us printers, of course, but we were looking for someone to be a lot more committed than that. Ryan, a summer intern in our office, came up with the idea of calling Printrbot, a small start-up that had raised their initial funds on Kickstarter and were selling a kind of do-it-yourself 3-D printer kits. We emailed Brook to see if he'd be interested in getting involved, and he emailed back the best response we had received yet. He said he had just watched my TED Talk—the one where I said, "If not now, then when? If not me, then who?"—and Brook said, "I have two words for you.

"Now. Me."

National Geographic was planning an issue on 3-D printing and heard about the project through a friend of mine, Dawn Rodney; they called to say they wanted to cover what we were doing. I told the guy who called that any press that we got involved in had to help inspire people to do they can do impossible things as well, and we wanted to reach people regardless of their socioeconomic status, their language, their religion, their color. And he said, "Well, how does thirty languages in thirty countries suit you, because that's the reach of *Nat Geo*?"

So, there was that, too.

◆

If the road to hell is paved with good intentions, then I should have known that that was the road we were on. Because everyone's intentions couldn't have been better. And everything was going as smooth as could be.

Until it wasn't.

Until I got an email from my contact at Intel that said, "We've got to talk."

There is nothing that will make you more nauseous than hearing the person who is in charge of giving you money for a project you're just weeks from launching half a world away say, "We've got to talk."

And sure enough, she told me that she was incredibly sorry, but her budget had been pulled. It was a long conversation, but it can be boiled down to two words.

We're out.

And so there I was. Marooned. Precipart had expressed interest in helping, but that's a long way from writing a check. And now Intel was out. I didn't know if I should call everyone and tell them that Project Daniel was in danger of collapsing, thus destroying whatever momentum we had, or if I should hold off and have everyone busting ass for a project that at the moment had a funding level of exactly nothing, which didn't seem fair.

I spent about twenty-four hours being Hamlet; I couldn't make up my mind what to do. I was depressed, but one thing I've learned about myself is that with the intensity and the optimism, the yang of doing, also comes the yin of facing defeat, the low, dark place, a place where I can't see the forest, I can't see the light, all I can see is that we're totally screwed.

So where does the Not Impossible concept come in when you're facing that dark place? How do you move from there? If the belief in the Not Impossible means that there is no giving up, how exactly do you get yourself to not give up?

For me, it's really kind of simple.

Being depressed is just too boring. It was like getting halfway through a jigsaw puzzle, and seeing it sitting there, half in pieces scattered around. It's just an ugly sight, and there's no pleasure in looking at it. So if you're selfish enough, and have little enough tolerance for boredom, there's only one choice, really.

Pick up the next piece, and figure out where it fits.

It was less than three weeks before I was scheduled to depart. Precipart had scheduled me to come in and talk to them about Project Daniel, but now my meeting was a little more urgent than I had thought. I had to shift the conversation from "excited to be involved with you guys" to "we have to do this NOW, guys." When you're making a pitch, it's important to find that very small place between a sense of urgency and a sense of desperation. I thought I'd found it—but my pitch didn't seem to be working. They were telling me, we'd love to help you, we are in, we are definitely in, but it's the end of the year, and for budgeting reasons we are not in a position to do that amount of money at this time. Later, no problem. But not right now.

The passion and commitment were there—but their checkbook was still in the pocket for another three months, which would be too late for Project Daniel.

The only one at Precipart who could save my ass at that moment was the last guy I thought would save my ass at that moment: the chairman, Lloyd Miller. Lloyd was a very buttoned-up, straitlaced kind of guy, who was listening quietly as everyone else spoke. He was very by-the-book, as far as I could tell. He ran a precision parts company, so one would hope he would be buttoned-up and by-the-book. I couldn't imagine him putting himself out for a project like this.

Which only goes to show how wrong you can be.

The next day, I was with Ollie, who told me the news: After I'd left, Lloyd had told everyone, excuse me, but we have to do this. And not only that: he said he would give up his own Christmas bonus to make it happen. And because of that, the project was green-lit.

I was blown away.

The lesson here, I guess, is that sometimes it's your own paranoia that makes you judge other people—that makes you think they're against you. I really do believe that every human being in this world is good, and if we don't see the good, then we're most likely misunderstanding them, and I am as capable as anyone else of doing the misunderstanding.

I had misunderstood Lloyd. I had judged him too soon. All of us in business have a cynical protective streak that says, a deal's not done until it's done and the ink is dry and the check is in your hand. But the downside of that caution is that you can walk into a situation prepared for things to fall apart, and that can become a self-fulfilling prophecy. If you walk in, as I did, saying, these people are engineers, by-the-book types, they're not risk-takers, then you make it too easy for them to live down to your expectations. What I took away from this encounter with Precipart was an understanding that if I can walk into a room and make everyone right in my mind, then there's a very good chance they'll live up to that positive potential that I see in them.

Ever since that day, when I look at someone and say, Oh, they'll never go for this pitch I'm making, I remind myself: There are no good monkeys, and there are no bad monkeys. There are only monkeys. Telling yourself something can't happen is a good way to make sure it doesn't. Remembering that people can surprise you, and will if you give them a chance, can give you the power to move forward.

To move mountains, in fact.

Because Lloyd Miller had just moved a mountain for me.

The day before I left for New York to meet with Precipart, I had called Will McGinniss, the executive creative director for Venables Bell, the advertising agency that works with Intel. Will and I were already friends from the advertising/production business, and I felt I could shoot straight with him. I told him, Intel is making a huge mistake here. This is going to be a massive story. The content that Intel is going to get for the amount they're paying—it's ridiculous. This time, I didn't try to find that little place between urgent and desperate—I just came on guns blazing, full force, saying, you have to change this.

And what do you know. He did.

I got back from meeting with Precipart on a Friday, and the very next day I heard from my contact at Intel. I knew that if they were calling me on Saturday, it had to be big. And I was right: Somehow, they'd found the money in the budget. Somehow, they were back on board.

And back on board in a big way: they came through with money, they came through with computers, and they came through with a solid commitment to stay with us through the project and beyond.

I learned later that this kind of roller-coaster ride is not unusual when you're trying to raise funds for an impossible project like this, but at the moment, I just felt like I had the bends. But in a good way, because we'd gone as low as we could go, and now we'd resurfaced.

Precipart made it possible, Intel was back in, and the local church diocese in the Nuba Mountains in Sudan was going to support us operationally, and—holy cow—we were back on.

We were headed to the Sudan.

We were off to find Daniel.

CHAPTER 10

If Not Now, When?

So what, exactly, were we headed into?

In the middle of all that was going on, Richard Van As weighed in to give us a dose of reality. I gotta say, it was a pretty hard pill to swallow.

In no uncertain terms, he warned us that going into a war zone would be much, much more dangerous than we could imagine. He told us that the moment we hit Sudan soil, we would become targets. That we would be kidnapped by rebels. And that we would witness the most unimaginable of horrors: "Gutting of pregnant women, hacking off breasts to those with little and newborn babies, execution-style shootings. They line up people and have fun . . . It is all in the name of terror."

I can't pretend that I wasn't scared to death by his email. I can't pretend that I didn't have second thoughts. And third. And fourth. And fifth. I certainly didn't share this email with my wife or anyone else close to me. In fact, Caskey is probably reading it here for the first time.

But somehow, the mission stayed with us and carried us through the doubt. I realized that I would be putting myself and the lives of my crew at risk. But I also knew that the kid we were focused on was just a kid, just like my kid, and there was no one around to help him, and his whole life depended on someone deciding to take that risk.

And so the mantra stayed with me:

If not now, then when?

If not me, then who?

◆

And so we decided to press on. We bought plane tickets and flew everyone to Los Angeles for a big meeting at my house. It was like the hacker weekend when we'd created the EyeWriter. There is something incredibly electric about putting everyone under one roof, of starting a project saying, this is not about my comfort, this is not about me in any way, this is just about getting the job done. Caskey, the kids, and I moved into one room, and we had to draw out a floor plan to figure out where everyone else was going to sleep.

We have a saying in the production business: it doesn't matter how much money or how little money you spend, all that matters is what shows up on the screen. That same philosophy was behind what we were doing here, only multiplied tenfold—it's the idea that every penny you have, and by extension every ounce of your energy and creativity and every bit of strength in your body, is geared toward getting the project over the finish line. And if you can engender that kind of attitude in your troops—well, then, nothing is impossible.

Which is, after all, the whole point.

So I fired up the pot for another session of spaghetti-making, and laid out a bunch of beer and chips, and once again the music was blaring, and the cameras were rolling, and the team was talking faster than most people can think.

Brook Drumm, the Printrbot guy, came along for the ride. So did David Putrino, another key member of the team, whom I had met up with in New York when I was pitching Precipart, just before the hack-a-thon weekend. David, an Australian native, is a world-class genius, a brain scientist, who was working on another project with us at the time. We had a cup of coffee, and when I told him what was going on with Project Daniel, he said, "You know, you're going to need a physical therapist."

Of course! He was right. I was so focused on the "maker" part of the process—the creation of the arm—I had totally forgotten about the human side, about the need to prepare someone physically to use a prosthetic, how to build up the muscles they'd need to operate it, how to protect them from pain at the intersection of man and machine.

I asked David if he knew a good physical therapist, and he said, "Just so happens, me." Turns out he was trained as a physical therapist before he became a genius brain scientist—some people just amaze you—and I heard these words coming out of my mouth: "David, I'm headed for the airport right now. Why don't I buy you a ticket and you come with me?"

And he said, "Why not?"

So then and there, in the coffee shop, on my phone, I purchased a ticket for him, and we were off to the races.

Once Richard Van As realized that we weren't giving up, even he agreed to fly in and give us a hand (literally and figuratively, of course). Dan Goodwin, an MIT guy, and a bunch of other hackers and makers and general geniuses and crazies, joined us, too.

And we set about the business of making arms.

Tim Freccia helped get everything set up in Sudan for our imminent arrival. He was the guy who made a million things work and was the critical first bit of momentum we needed on this project. Tim is one of those classic, tattooed, leather-skinned war photographers who's been everywhere, the kind of guy you love to have along on a mission like this, because he takes everything in stride and brings a "been there, done that" attitude, which at times is exactly what you need. And because he tells great stories. He was technically the photographer, but he was also the default producer-and-operations guy. One of the most important things he did was bring in a guy who I call Peter the Slow-talking Englishman. Peter Moszynski was going to be our fixer, the guy who arranges everything. Peter walks with a cane and a slight limp but never seems to lose a step. He's an enormously detailed, incredibly focused individual—in other words, the exact opposite of me—who mapped out the logistics of the trip, step by step.

We also brought in Adrian Belic, the Academy Award–nominated director, to film the whole experience. I felt it was very important to have a film crew record the trip, because communicating to the world that something like this was not impossible was central to our mission. And you couldn't find a better person to do it than Adrian.

Adrian had directed a documentary titled *Beyond the Call,* about three middle-aged former soldiers who travel the world, delivering humanitarian aid to doctors on or behind the front lines of war-torn countries. He seemed like a natural for Project Daniel. In fact, this will tell you all you need to know about Adrian: When we called him up and told him about the project, he said yes, immediately. Yes, I'll come to the Sudan with you. Yes, I'll risk my life to help tell this story. Yes, I'm in.

It wasn't until about three days later that he asked me, Oh, by the way, is there any money in this? Like, do I actually get paid?

That's the kind of guy he is. And that's how this whole thing works. People commit because something in them says they have to. We did pay Adrian, of course, but it was clear that he would have been in either way.

The first night of the get-together, as folks were planning how to get the 3-D printers to work, and how many screws and strings we were going to need to ship to the Sudan, and what modifications we thought we should make to Richard's arm, and how many pounds of equipment each plane would allow us—those millions of details that I'm lucky other people are good at—I pulled Adrian aside and, for the first time, expressed the fear that I was trying not to feel.

"Talk to me a little bit," I asked him. "Are you a little bit freaked out at all about the safety of where we're going?"

And he started to laugh.

He told me how many times he'd gone into the worst situations to film *Beyond the Call* with the three crazy ex-military guys who were out to become modern-day knights, saving the world and ignoring their own safety. He rattled off the places they'd been: Afghanistan. Rwanda. Burma. Albania. Chechnya. Cambodia.

Suddenly, I felt like the rookie in the room. But it was okay, because the message was clear.

You wanna save the world?

You gotta leave the house.

An early prototype during the Maker weekend for
Project Daniel.

I was feeling really good about the whole thing. With all this brainpower surrounding me, what, I thought, could possibly go wrong?

Turns out, everything.

We didn't actually make any arms that weekend. We tried, though. A friend of mine, Tom Dunlap, hooked us up with one of the most well-known amputees in the country, Sarah Herron. Sarah was born without one arm but grew up to become a beautiful, confident young woman who appeared on the TV show *The Bachelor*. She agreed to come over to let us try to make an arm for her.

Once these sweaty, smelly, panting guys who'd been sleeping on the floor for two days got over the shock of having this knockout blonde walk through the door, we got to work. And not to put too fine a point on it, it was a total disaster. She was incredibly kind about it, but it was a train wreck from the start. We tried attaching the arm by taking a piece of PVC pipe and heating it up and putting it around the stump of her arm. It just wouldn't work. And the 3-D printers weren't working right, either. We just kept having misprint after misprint. To make matters worse, she was missing her left arm, and the only versions we had printed were right arms.

But that's part of the Not Impossible process—you have to see each of those setbacks not as a failure, but as a teaching moment. You have to think, hey, this is lucky, I made all these mistakes now, so I don't have to make them when I get to Africa.

In the end, all the problems were ultimately the result of the various versions of prosthetics that everyone brought to the table for the Maker weekend. The difficulty was that no one except Richard had any experience with the nuances of prosthetics, so in the end we pretty much went with the core of what Richard had created, and that did the trick.

Richard himself got so frustrated with us that he walked out—he went back to South Africa early because he thought we just couldn't get our act together.

But he didn't stay off the project for very long.

Once a train like this starts rolling, it's hard to jump off.

◆

Even though the money for the trip had managed to fall into place, over the next couple of weeks, some of the crew was falling out.

My plan was that I would go as the ringleader, and we'd have two people on the tech side and a small film crew. The film crew held together. But the tech side fell apart. One of the guys who we had lined up to help work the 3-D printers and make the arms had been really enthusiastic and kept saying, I'm in! I'm in! I'm in!—but he called me a week before the trip and said, "I'm out."

"Out?" I said, incredulous. "What do you mean, out?"

"I've been reading a lot of stuff," he said. "It's too dangerous over there. My girlfriend said she'd break up with me if I went."

Another techie also told me that he couldn't travel with us—he desperately wanted to, but couldn't. So now I had no one on the tech side. Just me. All alone. And I'd barely ever used a 3-D printer. I thought, no way I could possibly do this myself.

Or could I?

There comes a moment when the bomb goes off and you look around at the rubble and you're standing all alone, that postapocalyptic moment we've all experienced at one time or another—when everything you're working on just goes to hell—and you have to make a decision. You either lie down in the rubble or you start walking. It's not easy—it's almost like you have to go through the five stages of grief: the denial, anger, bargaining, depression, and acceptance—but it's a moment that defines you.

Then it occurred to me. I thought, you know, I'm looking for someone fearless, someone who's too impatient to look at the details of why this won't work, someone who's gonna get on a plane and not question the whole idea, someone who lives his life with reckless abandon. Where, I thought, am I gonna find a stupid bastard like that?

And the answer came back: If not now, then when? If not me, then who?

From that moment, I started doing something I learned from Father Becker, my nutty English teacher at Brophy College Prep, my Jesuit high school in Phoenix. He used to talk endlessly about the Power of Tenses. And I used that, when folks at my office started saying I was crazy for even thinking of doing this—I started talking about it in the past tense. I said, "When I decided to do this," or,

"When we began this trip"—like it was already done. It helped them get their heads around it—it made it real for them, like a thing that has already happened.

And in some ways it had. Because suddenly, once I'd accepted the reality of the idea—that I would go on the trip with no other tech people; that I'd be the sole maker—it was almost like the universe decided that it agreed with me, and began aligning itself along this new reality.

Out of the blue, Richard Van As, the Robohand expert, called me up from Johannesburg. Mind you, this is the same Richard Van As, the grumpiest guy on the planet, who scolded me for even thinking about going to the Sudan and who said I'd never get ready in time. The same Richard who had walked out of our hacker weekend because he thought we didn't have our act together.

When I told him that it was just me going to Sudan now, he said, "Look, come to Johannesburg on your way to the Sudan. Stay with me. I'll train you to do it all."

I almost dropped the phone. So there you go. I'd have five or maybe even six whole days to become an expert in printing and attaching prosthetic arms. How hard could that be?

From there, other pieces of the puzzle started magically falling into place as well. While Daniel had been the inspiration for this project—you have to help one before you can help many—we knew that we might never find him. Or even if he were still alive. There was such chaos in Sudan, there was no guarantee we'd be able to locate one refugee out of the hundreds of thousands of them. We'd resolved to continue with the quest, whether or not we did actually find him. But we Skyped with Dr. Catena one night, and lo and behold, he had found Daniel in a 65,000-person refugee camp in Sudan called Yida. The same camp the UN says is "the most challenging refugee camp in the world."

The politics of Sudan are horrendous and horrendously complicated. But the root of it is the civil war that had been going on in this nation in northeast Sub-Saharan Africa. Ever since Colonel Omar al-Bashir took over the government in a coup in 1989, with the purpose of creating an undisputed Islamic state and purging all non-Islamic figures from the government, things have gotten worse and worse. The killings carried out in Bashir's name, either by the army or by the militant Janjaweed associated with him, were quickly characterized as genocide by the international community. In Darfur alone, the troubled region on which Bashir unleashed the most vicious of his murderous troops, more than a half million people have died in what the UN has called one of the worst humanitarian disasters in the world. Yep, the horrors of Darfur were caused by Bashir. And yep, I was headed into Bashir territory.

The fighting between the government forces of the despot Bashir and the rebels who opposed his bloody regime didn't end with a peace agreement in the mid-2000s, which eventually led to the creation of the new nation of South Sudan. In some ways, the violence intensified, and much of it shifted to the border area of the Nuba Mountains, which were technically part of Sudan but currently under the control of the rebels. The main rebel group was the Sudan People's Liberation Army, the SPLA; a break-off faction of that group, the SPLA-North or SPLA-N, was operating in the Nuba Mountains.

That summer, just before we left for Africa, there had been many terrible reports of atrocities. Bashir had started bombing civilians in the several contested areas, mainly the Nuba Mountains, at an alarming rate.

Our plan was to get into the new nation of South Sudan and cross the northern border illegally into Sudan by night, aided by SPLA-N. Somehow, they had adopted the project (thank you, Peter the Slow-talking Englishman). We also had the support of a nongovernmental organization that operates anonymously, and the church diocese that supports Dr. Catena—none of which made me feel any less terrified about what we were planning to do.

It was early October, the original planned start date, although we had already pushed the date for the trip back to November. I was thinking of pushing the trip back one more month to December so that I'd have time to raise more money and get things a little more in order. But Peter called and said, You don't understand, I've never seen anything in Africa line up this well and this precisely. And nothing lasts forever. Things are working in this moment—that doesn't mean they'll be working in the next.

In other words, get your butt out the door right now.

So we picked a date, packed our bags, and headed for the unknown to try to do the impossible.

CHAPTER 11

Help One, Help Many

Turbulence woke me up in the middle of the night on my flight to Johannesburg, and I could not stop thinking about Daniel. He was like some mythical being I was going to meet. I wondered: Is his family still alive? Who does he live with now? What is his attitude? Is he a positive person? In the light and the face of all the horrors he's seen, he might not be. And he wouldn't have any reason to. There's no reason on earth that he would be holding out hope of a better life. But does he? What will he think of this six-foot-six bald white American stepping into his world? Will he be open to these contraptions? And will they even work? Will this be as big of a failure as it had been with Sarah?

I'd never spoken to Daniel. It had been two weeks since Dr. Catena located him, and I was just hoping that he would still be locatable once we got there. I was anxious. I was nervous. I felt like a mail-order bride being shipped halfway around the world to meet the person I was destined to be with. It felt like there was an element of fate to all of this: that Daniel happened to be the person about whom that article was written; that I happened to read that article about him; that I happened to meet the people who knew the doctor who treated him. I don't care what religion you are, or aren't—you can't feel like that's all just chance. You can't feel that when it's the middle of the night, and you're on a turbulent flight to Johannesburg, anyway.

The turbulence had been crazy. Glasses were flying, people were letting out little gasps and shrieks, food was everywhere. But the

145

stewardesses were unflappable—just going about their business, as though turbulence was the most natural thing in the world.

There was a good lesson for me in that. See the calm in the center of the turbulence. I was praying that I could remember it throughout this trip.

The turbulence died down, but I couldn't get back to sleep, so I turned to the book I was reading, *They Poured Fire on Us from the Sky*, the story of three of the Lost Boys of Sudan, the thousands of little boys from the Dinka tribe who were orphaned during the war, the brutality they witnessed, the horrors they lived through. Somehow, knowing that I was going to that land, that I was going to meet some of those very same boys, made the reality of what they had lived through even more terrifying. To see your parents killed right before your eyes, to travel barefoot for a thousand miles, starving, dying of thirst, seeing your friends blown apart by land mines or eaten by crocodiles or carried off by lions—my God. And all to reach a refugee camp to live a life that is only less harsh by a matter of a few degrees, if that.

Two million people have already died as a result of the brutality brought on by the regime of Omar al-Bashir. Two million. It is impossible to grasp. Hundreds of thousands more have been wounded, children left orphaned in numbers that stagger the imagination. Fifty thousand amputees. One of the bloodiest wars Africa has ever known. A holocaust, happening as we speak.

The only way to come to grips with these numbers is to hear the story of one group of boys, which is why I was reading this book. And the only way I know to start to deal with it is to try to help one boy. Which is why I was traveling to find Daniel. Of course, I hoped with all my heart that what I was doing would wind up helping more than one boy. But that's the only way I could think about it. I could help many only by helping one first.

As I read about one of the Lost Boys, I keep thinking, I want my sons to meet Daniel. I want to have him over to dinner. I want my boys to know how incredibly privileged they are. I want them to see what the rest of the world can be like.

◆

I call South Africa the Land of Tall Fences. Almost every house in Johannesburg has a ten-foot fence around it, with another three or four feet of electrical wire or barbed wire above that. It feels a little like you're living in a zoo.

I felt that way even more once I stepped inside Richard's home in Johannesburg, because there were animals everywhere: two Rottweilers, a giant tortoise, a big parrot, a bunch of cats. The Rottweilers were massive, and must have been one hundred pounds if they weighed an ounce. One of them, Karma, was very sweet, with a little puppy face, but the other, Rocco, was a stone-cold killer. Every time you walked by, he just kind of seized up and stared at you like he'd love to rip your neck out.

Which of the dogs represented what this trip was going to be like for me, I didn't want to begin to guess.

Outside the house there were two fountains, a swath of beautiful low trees, and bougainvillea a shade of purple I've never seen in my life. Across the street, beyond the six-foot stone wall with its six electric wires, a huge shantytown had grown up. It's what they euphemistically call an "unplanned settlement" here, and it would seem strange to be in such a nice house in the midst of such poverty if it weren't so completely common. But I didn't focus on it much; Richard and the film team and I all said our hellos, and almost immediately I set up our printers and got to work.

If you've never seen 3-D printing, imagine someone writing "happy birthday" on a cake, in frosting, squeezing the frosting out of a tube. Only after you make the *H*, you write it again, in precisely the same place as the first letters, again and again, until you have a big 3-D *H* on your cake. On a 3-D printer, the heated tube is called an extruder, and the icing—called the filament—starts out like a strand of hard spaghetti. After the filament is heated by the extruder, it comes out like a strand of gelatinous goo, and then hardens almost immediately into the firm plastic shape that you set out to print. What you can draw with a 3-D printer is limited only by your imagination: for the most part, if you can think it, you can make it.

The great thing about 3-D printing is that it represents what is called rapid prototyping: You don't have to spend a lot of time overthinking things. You design something on the computer screen, you hit Print, and you can hold your design in your hands, often in just a matter of hours. If you want to share what you're making with somebody five thousand miles away, you can just send them a file as easily as you send your mother a picture of your kids, and they can print the same file on their 3-D printer, and you're both looking at the same exact physical object at the same time.

That's the good part. The bad part is, when you screw up, you find out about it really quick. Jet-lagged, I stayed up that whole first night, getting the printers going, tweaking the settings, and print-ing some test hand parts. I made a lot of mistakes. That was great, I kept telling myself, because each mistake was a part of my learning process, and better to make them here in Johannesburg, where I had help, than later when I was on my own in Sudan.

It's really an ingenious device, the hand that Richard devised. Basically, the hand attached to the stump of an amputee's arm, so that when he flexes his elbow, it pulls on a series of strings attached to the fingers and thumb, causing them to make a kind of pinching or grabbing motion.

The hardest part of the process was already done for me—Richard had figured out the logic and engineering of how the arm works, and created the 3-D files, and made arms and proved that they work. From there, it was really just as simple as hitting Print.

Each section of the hand is printed separately: the palm, which everything is mounted on, and the fingers and thumb, which each come out in two parts. We bolted those all together, and then started adding the strings that connect the fingers to the motion of the arm.

As the sun came up, smoke was rising from the paraffin stoves of the shantytown across the street, giving everything an eerie, otherworldly feel—as though being surrounded by a half dozen disembodied plastic hands didn't do that trick already. I was feeling as tired as I've ever felt.

And as alive as I've ever felt, too.

◆

Tim Freccia, the photographer who would document the trip, showed up the next day. The first day he was there, we sat down to eat a fine lamb stew, and he told us about visiting an ambassador's house in another country. It was all white linen tablecloths and fine silverware, but the plates came out with tiny carcasses on them, and he realized, oh, damn, we're about to eat rat. The other guests around the table dug in and said how good it was, and, not wanting to be the ugly American who's above the native culture, he started eating it, too. And it was horrible.

"This," he deadpanned, raising a spoonful of his lamb stew, "is much better."

That first afternoon Tim was there, he started playing with a drone, which we had brought along so we could get some over-head shots when we got to Sudan. While he did that, I got back to working on the arms. It was scary to think that in a few days I'd be leaving for Sudan where I was going to have to make them on my own and figure out how to teach other people to do it, too, so they could keep it going after I left. I felt the kind of scared that grabs you by the scrotum and doesn't let go but sure keeps you awake and alert and alive. I shadowed Richard all afternoon in the cramped workshop, watching him work, trying to copy every movement he made, getting his process down. Almost like watching a prizefighter and trying to mimic his footwork and jabs.

I wanted to get to the point where I could make an arm, start to finish, in twelve hours, and teach somebody to do the same. My dream was that it could become a little microbusiness for somebody in Sudan. You know, maybe they'd just earn couple of shekels, but it would be a couple more shekels than they had before they started.

Richard is very intense. I'd nicknamed him Captain Grumpy and brought him a T-shirt from home with two of Snow White's dwarves on it and the words, "I'm Grumpy because you're Dopey."

Richard's attitude reminded me of what my dad used to say: Come on, don't whine about it, just do it. It doesn't take any longer to do it right than it does to do it wrong, so you might as well do it right, don't you think?

But I didn't mind. For one thing, you can't get around the fact that the man is making, with his own money, hand after hand after hand for people with disabilities whether they can afford it or not. It's pretty incredible. And for another thing, every hour that went by brought me an hour closer to the moment that I'd have to do all this on my own, when I'd be flying without a net. So if I had to choose between Richard being polite and Richard cramming as much information into my head as he possibly could in two days, I'll take the information, thank you very much.

On our first day in Johannesburg, I'd watched Richard fit a young boy named Celio with a new hand. I heard his story: a few years back, a car speeding by had flipped and landed on top of him. He had been stuck under the car for three hours. When they finally got the car off of him, his hand had been totally destroyed. He'd lived as an amputee ever since.

When Celio came for his first fitting, it was electrifying for me, even though I'd seen Richard making hands since I'd arrived, and I'd known about the process for months. But now there was a boy, an actual person, Celio, who needed this hand more than most people I know have ever needed anything. Now that the "one" in "help one, help many" had arrived on the scene, everything had changed. Suddenly this was not about 3-D printers and extruders and bolts and fittings. This was about a boy. I sat quietly as Richard warmed the orthoplastic—a solid but flexible material that you can put in boiling water to soften and then shape to the contours of the stump. I watched how he formed it with his hands, molding the contours to Celio's stump.

I wondered what it would feel like, for me, when I made my first hand for someone. I didn't have to wait long. Richard had something up his sleeve. Something he hadn't told me about, but that I'd find out about soon enough.

◆

That night, after Richard's whip-smart and lovely wife, Beth, and his incredibly polite and conscientious daughters laid out another fabulous dinner for us, I sat outside and listened to the sounds of the shantytown across the street. It's a massive community, and the sound was so full of life and laughter, it just filled my heart.

As I sat there, cars zipped by, filled with teenagers, the windows down, blaring rap music, rock music, all kinds of music. I think that's something universal, across cultures, across skin color, across national boundaries: young boys, fast cars, windows down, music loud.

It occurred to me at that moment that the urge to help people is just as universal. It crosses cultural boundaries, physical boundaries, time, and space itself. Rich, poor, it doesn't matter: Helping someone feels good. It makes you happy.

I was a big reader of Ayn Rand a few years back and became a big believer in the theory of selfishness. When I told somebody that, they said, Hey, I never took you for a right-winger. I was taken aback, because I guess I was just blind to the fact that a lot of people who happen to be Republicans take Ayn Rand as a philosophical model—but for me, the theory of selfishness is something totally outside of politics. When I created the EyeWriter, it just felt good, and I said to myself, Hey, I want more of this. For me, creating something that helps someone else is an addictive feeling.

And that's what Ayn Rand said to me: Her theory of selfishness is the very definition of altruism. If you want to do good in the world, be selfish. Do what makes you feel good, and that will wind up helping everyone else. The desire to help is something real and inherent and alive and universal. It's like what kept my mom doing her chaplain work, even while she was holding down two jobs to help support the family: Helping others just gave her joy.

What makes you feel good? Making pancakes for your kids in the morning? Waking up, having a cup of coffee, mixing the batter, pouring it into the pan, flipping it over, watching your kids' faces when you plop it on their plates, lingering a minute to see the intensity with which they carefully spread the butter, or the syrup, or the whipped cream, because it's that important to them that they get it right, because they like it so much when it's just right.

Now let's say a robber came and stole your mixing bowl, your spatula, your flour and eggs and baking powder. Now you can't make the pancakes for your kids. You can't have that selfish pleasure, and they lose out as well. You just want to have that pleasure back—and by being selfish, by running out and getting new supplies because you want to feel good, you're helping your kids out as well, because now they get to have their favorite breakfast again.

It's not that complicated.

I was missing my own kids, sitting there knowing that as the afternoon wore on in Johannesburg, it was the morning of Halloween back home. We throw a big Halloween party every year; the whole neighborhood shows up, and Caskey, true to her Mexican roots, always has a giant piñata stuffed with creepy Halloween toys. But this year—for the first time ever—Caskey would be throwing the party without me. It was the first Halloween I had ever missed with my kids.

When I Skyped with them, they were as excited as hell, and the Halloween party was just starting. Trace was dressed as the Big Bad Wolf, Angus was a Vampire Macklemore, and Bo was some creation

My three sons, on the first Halloween I ever missed.

of his own imagination known as the Grim Reaper's brother. It was killing me not to be there. I had a sick feeling in the pit of my stomach because I knew I could never replace that moment with my boys. I knew I would never get a three-year-old Big Bad Wolf again.

I distracted myself by working in the workshop until nearly dawn, then caught a few hours' sleep. When I woke up, I heard some commotion outside. I got dressed and went down to see what was going on.

Richard was outside with a young man who was missing one hand. His arm had been amputated below the elbow.

"This is Gideon," Richard said. "Mick, you're going to make him a hand. See you guys later."

I introduced myself and felt kind of awkward. For all the planning and talking and technical aspects of this project, this was my first time dealing with an actual human being for whom I was going to make a hand. There was a part of me that felt as though Gideon was trying to put me at ease, rather than the other way around. We talked and joked for a while, through a translator, and Gideon told me his story. He had been involved in a hit-and-run accident; he was working on a mining crew, and a drunk driver hit him and left him in a ditch. By the time he was found and brought to the hospital, the arm was beyond saving. Like a lot of people, he fought the amputation, but they told him, Look, this hand will not heal, and it will kill you. You have to do this.

Until I'd arrived in Johannesburg, I had never been in the presence of anyone—other than Richard—who had had to make that decision. Soon I would be in the presence of dozens, maybe hundreds, maybe thousands of young boys and girls who had been faced with that same agonizing choice. And others who never even had the choice at all. Richard had realized that I needed to work on someone, a real person, before going to Sudan. He understood that printing an arm in a lab would be very different from the reality of making and fitting an arm for a person in the field.

As my good friend Ubi likes to say, this shit just got real.

As Gideon and I talked, I attached a prototype hand onto his arm, just so he'd get the feel of it—not that he'd be able to work it yet, but just so that he could use the thumb to pick up something that had a handle. Then I grabbed a bucket and placed it on the ground in front of Gideon. Tentatively, he reached down with his plastic hand, hooked the fingers under the bucket handle, and started to lift. Slowly, slowly, the bucket rose, until it was even with his face, which burst into the most ridiculously wide grin I've ever seen.

Fitting Gideon for the arm was a long, slow process. We'd brought about four hundred dollars' worth of orthoplastic with us, which I'd thought would solve all our problems. It was super cheap, had the best breathability, and wasn't going to get messed up by the sweat from your skin. But when we tested it out, it was just too malleable, too flexible. So the fitting process was a lot slower and clumsier than I'd hoped it would be. Gideon was incredibly patient, but as the hours ticked by, I could tell he was getting bored. I had an idea about how to keep him in the game.

"Gideon," I said to him, as a few folks gathered to see how it was going, "I need you to put this hand on, so I can see how it's fitting." He complied.

"Okay, now I just need to test some functionality. Can you touch your right shoulder with your left arm?" He did. "Now the right arm to the left shoulder." Again, he complied. I walked him through the next steps—right arm to the side of the head, followed by the left; right arm to left hip; left arm to right hip. And just as he was looking like, what is wrong with this big white guy, I yelled, "Hey, Macarena!"

Everybody started cracking up, and someone started singing a la-la-la version of "Macarena," and we were all wiggling around and doing the dance; apparently some song crazes are worldwide, or maybe getting punked is funny for a young man, no matter what the culture, because Gideon started laughing like I hadn't heard him laugh all morning. He made me run through the joke again, and it was just as funny the second time. Maybe funnier.

We wound up buying some better orthoplastic from Richard's supplier, and I got the whole setup about right, and Gideon tried on his new device. Richard wandered by to see how things were going. Gideon walked over to a table that had a little green Nerf football sitting on it and—as though he'd been doing it all his life—put his hand over the ball, bent his elbow so the strings made his fingers clench around the Nerf ball, and, ever so slowly, and ever so perfectly, picked it up.

That moment set my heart ablaze. The moment that someone who you just met, who is missing the hand on his left arm, suddenly has one that works, fires every synapse in your brain. No drug, no sex, no rock and roll, no food, no drink, no experience—nothing compares to this moment of having created something so simple and yet so profound—out of nothing, out of a bunch of liquid plastic and a few strings and some cheap bolts from the hardware store, you have given someone a new lease on life.

To see Gideon playing with the new hand was a lovely, and startling, and astounding feeling. This was not about me, this was about him, and I tried not to act like Mister Look What I Did, but I'm sure I couldn't hide the pride I felt in that moment. And as crusty and grumpy as Richard is, I could tell how much he loved teaching people to help people, and in that moment, he was beaming at me like a proud papa at a Little League game whose kid just knocked one out of the park.

We took Gideon out to Richard's backyard to interview him, and I was really surprised by what he said. He told me that the thing he looked forward to the most was going out and socializing again. We asked him why he thought the hand would let him do that.

He explained that, unlike a lot of the amputees he'd met, he had remained pretty functional; he was getting by okay with one hand. Physically, anyway. Emotionally, it was another story.

"I don't really go out," he told me, "because I'm embarrassed. You know, you wear a long-sleeved shirt or a jacket, and it just hangs there and looks weird."

I hadn't thought of that—I was so caught up in the functionality of the hand, it never occurred to me that it could become—as Gideon was explaining it—a positive social tool, too.

"People are going to want to see how it works, to check it out," Gideon said. "It'll be cool."

Yes, I thought. This is all very, very cool.

◆

Late that afternoon, a South African storm rolled in. Just before the rain broke the sky was the darkest gray, but it melded down at sunset to a bright pinkish-orange with striations of blue above the black hills that were illuminated by the dim lights of streetlamps. It felt like an omen of some kind, like one of those moments you have to pay attention to because something important is going to happen. A few moments later, the rain started, heavy and relentless, big fat raindrops hitting the pavement and bouncing, pounding on the roof with a sound like the sizzling of bacon in a pan. We were planning a barbecue that night, and I figured, well, that's off, but Richard's friends and family who were arranging the barbecue didn't even blink an eye; they just moved their stuff a few feet, edged it under a little canopy, and just kept on. It was a teaching moment, for me: a simple experience of the African way of life, of stepping around adversity and just keeping on.

The dinner was exquisite—the barbecued beef was incredible, and Richard's wife, Beth, had made the best French fries I've ever had—but I kept thinking about the barbecue in the rain and how easily they'd kept the barbecue going once the rain had started.

It was exactly what I had felt from Gideon that day, but hadn't been able to express to myself: Although he said he had fought, at first, against what was happening to him, by the time I met him he'd accepted it, adapted to it, overcome it. What I had done was just one more step in the process that began for him the moment his arm was amputated: a process of advancing, of overcoming. I felt very blessed, and very lucky, to be exposed to these people of such indomitable spirit—I knew that Gideon was, in a way, a harbinger for me, a beginning. That there would be many, many more Gideons to meet in Sudan, on glorious days, days of creation and sunset, and darkness and light, and resilience and fortitude.

And, if you're lucky, a good dinner at the end.

◆

That night, at 2:00 a.m., everyone was asleep but me. I needed to sleep, because we were leaving for Sudan the next day, but I couldn't. I had printed all of one arm solo in my life and was about to venture into the most uncharted territory of my life to do something I'd barely learned to do, so any more minutes of practice I could squeak in would be golden. So I got up and went to Richard's workshop and began puttering away.

I hadn't been sleeping that much anyway, since I got to Johannesburg. It was pretty much: crash, get up, brush your teeth, walk into the workshop, go all day long and late into the night, grab a couple of hours of sleep, and start it all again. Because there are only so many hours to learn to do all these things.

I sat at a desk that was scattered with tools and drills and plastic hands and 3-D printing mistakes. There was dust everywhere and no sound but the hum and the drone of the 3-D printers and the glow of the computer screens. It was really quite nippy after the storm—I hadn't expected a cold spell in Africa, so I hadn't brought the right clothes, and most of the clean stuff I had was packed up and ready to go, so I was sitting there in surf trunks and a T-shirt, printing hands and freezing my ass off.

I took some solace in the fact that Richard only started doing this in January of 2013, and I started in October 2013, so I was really only a couple of months behind him—and he was the inventor and the sensei master of the Robohand. I tried to keep that perspective. And I also reflected on a great conversation I'd had with Richard earlier that night. He doesn't drink, but he pulled out a bottle of cognac, and we raised a toast to each other. Richard is not given to big shows of emotion, so I was startled when he raised his little shot of cognac and said, "You're going to do fine, my friend. I wish I were going with you."

I was taken aback. This was the same gruff, grumpy guy who'd lectured me about how I shouldn't go. For Richard to say he believed I could do it, and wished he could come with me, was about the highest praise I could have hoped for.

Again, I'm not about external praise—I think confidence in yourself has to come from yourself. But every once in a while—especially coming from someone you respect, as much as I did Richard—it's still nice to hear.

Fail, Fail, Fail, Succeed.
Repeat as Necessary.

The first thing I noticed about Juba was the mosquitoes.

The rains that had moved through the capital the night before we got there had left a million mosquitoes in their wake. We were setting up lights to do a few interviews, and the sound of the mosquitoes buzzing and zapping around the hot lights was strange and disorienting.

Juba is an island amid an impoverished Third World scene: crowded streets, cars and motorbikes honking like mad at each other, potholes the size of craters everywhere, and, due to the political situation, more Toyota Land Rovers with international or United Nations plates than you can imagine. It was very intense. We were scheduled to stay for two days, get ourselves organized, pick up the rest of the supplies we needed, and head on to Yida, the refugee camp.

A few hours after we arrived in Juba, there was going to be a solar eclipse—which felt like an omen of some kind, though I didn't want to think too long about what—and someone arranged to take us on a boat trip on the Nile River to watch it. It was a surreal experience, to be riding in a car through those impoverished streets, surrounded by the hustle and bustle of people dressed in rags, trying to eke out a living, and suddenly to find yourself on a boat on the Nile loaded with Germans sipping on beers and a young Sudanese guy playing the bongos, with a focus and relentlessness that would have been impressive if he were not so thoroughly lacking in any sense of rhythm or beat. It was kind of psychedelic, trying to shift from one scene to the other so quickly. And it just kept getting stranger: We passed a small island in the middle of the Nile, and there by the shore was a young kid, sleeping under a seventy-foot-tall mango tree, on a trampoline. There was nothing else on the island, no structures—just the trampoline. It was like something out of a Fellini movie: What the hell is a trampoline doing on an island in the Nile?

We docked on that same island, near the kid on the trampoline, bathed in the glow of the light of the eclipse, and the Germans popped open another beer. I was overcome with a terrible sense of Catholic guilt, knowing we were having this incredibly luxurious moment in the midst of such poverty. But in two days, I didn't know where I'd sleep, what I'd be eating, and whether I'd already be in the throes of malaria, since I'd never had so many mosquito bites in my whole life. So I figured, better enjoy the moment while the moment's here.

Which is, of course, another important lesson I brought back.

◆

Our hotel, the aptly named Bedouin Hotel, was pretty rustic, to say the least, although I gathered it was palatial by Juba standards. There were about twenty palapas, basically little huts that looked like work sheds, but they had running water and soft beds and mosquito nets and electricity, so we felt pretty lucky, in spite of an awful smell coming from next door. The hotel was right next to a butcher facility, and in the daytime, they burn the horns of the cows, which gives off a terrible pungent odor. They burn frankincense in the hotel all day, just to try to keep the smell a little bit manageable, but if you're not used to the smell of bull horn and frankincense, it's still pretty horrible.

On our first full day in Juba, we were doing errands, screaming through town in the back of pickup trucks, dodging potholes the size of a VW Beetle, getting our press passes (which would permit us to move about the country), all guided by our driver, Ken, who was hired by Peter to help arrange the whole trip.

At one point when we stopped, I mentioned to Ken that I was wondering about Daniel, whether he was alive, whether we'd find him, how much I was looking forward to meeting him. "Oh," Ken said. "I have some footage of Daniel. Do you think you wanna see it?"

After all this time, after all this preparation, it never occurred to me that somebody might actually have video of Daniel. So that night, after dinner, we got together in one of the huts, and Ken played it for us on his laptop. I wasn't really expecting anything—just a chance to see Daniel, to hear his voice, that sort of thing.

Oh my God.

The video was a Channel 4 report, filed by reporter Aidan Hartley, who'd gained unprecedented access to the Nuba Mountains area, escorted by the Sudan People's Liberation Army of the North. Ken clicked forward to the point in the video where Hartley makes his way to the hospital where Dr. Tom Catena held forth. As I watched, Dr. Catena was removing the bandages from Daniel's arms after the amputations. Even in the video, I could see in Daniel's eyes the sense of hurt, of resignation, of sadness. He refused to speak and didn't seem to be making eye contact with anyone. It was heartbreaking.

And it was just the beginning.

Ken clicked back to the beginning of the video, where Hartley was making his way through the Nuba Mountains, the stronghold of the rebel SPLA-N and the main focus of Bashir's brutal bombing campaign. I'd read about what was going on, and cognitively I understood it, or thought I did, but to see it, with my own eyes, was way different.

It was the first time, I have to be honest, that I really understood the horror of Sudan. My stomach started to churn as I watched the children—no older than my own boys—hiding in caves when they heard the whine of approaching Antonov planes, followed by the inevitable explosion of the bombs they dropped. Here was a family of five, who only had leaves to eat. Here were children cowering in foxholes as death rained down all around them.

At a school—not a schoolhouse, because there was no building, but a school—more than a hundred children assembled among a grove of acacia trees. They were singing a song and preparing for the day when one of them heard the sound of a bomber and screamed. Suddenly hundreds of children were fleeing for their lives, hiding in a nearby cave.

It's a scene that will stay with me for a long time.

The tape returned to the scene with Dr. Catena again, and I watched again as he removed the gauze from Daniel's arms. It went on to show other casualties: A woman who lost her arm in an explosion that claimed the life of her mother. And two of her sisters. And her baby. A teenage boy who had half his face blown away by a bomb. Dr. Catena had saved his life, but he would be terribly disfigured, forever.

Dr. Catena said that he'd already operated on more than seven hundred people with severe war casualties. More than 80 percent, he estimated, were civilians.

Why, the reporter asked him, didn't he flee when this latest round of bombings started? Why on earth had he stayed in a place where he faced such certain danger?

"I guess the way I see it is there is not another option," he said. "What are your options? You leave and abandon everybody here, or you stay and you go ahead. That's the only other option."

In other words, if not now, when? If not me, who?

His words stayed with me as I packed up for the night. I was shaken by what I'd seen. It's one thing to read about the horror and the devastation, it's another to see it with your own eyes.

And in forty-eight hours, I would be there.

◆

The next morning we woke up and started sorting out our gear. Our remarkable friend, Peter the Slow-talking Englishman, was there early, to get things organized. Peter has been involved with Sudan for more than thirty years; many of the people who are in office right now were Peter's students when they were kids. I thought of him as the Obi-Wan Kenobi who was going to lead us into battle; I have no idea what kind of Jedi mind tricks he uses to get things done, but he makes things happen and gets doors that seem sealed shut to open. When I saw how much he had lined up for us, and how it was all coming together, I could only sit back and be thankful.

We'd left America not knowing how we were getting our gear to Yida, because there are severe weight restrictions on luggage on the planes. Somehow Peter had gotten us permission to transport 250 kilos worth of gear—about 550 pounds. And it's a good thing, because between the printers, all the plastic filament, and our camera equipment, we needed every ounce we could get. The gear was supposed to leave before we did, and, frankly, I was more anxious about being separated from our gear than anything else—although, if I'd been thinking clearly, I should've been more anxious about getting our heads blown off than anything else. I have Tim, the wartime photographer, and Adrian Belic, the videographer, and Peter to thank for that. They'd spent enough time in war zones to develop an ability to focus on the task at hand and block out the bigger picture, which is essential to getting anything like this done. In a way, focus is part of the philosophy we'd been developing at Not Impossible— if you want to help many, help one. Blocking out the big picture and deciding to just help one kid—just help Daniel—was making it possible for me to move forward.

Even though we had a common goal, there was some tension among the members of the team. But it was a good tension that came from the passion everyone had for the project, for wanting to get it done and get it done right. That's essential for a manager to be able to discern, I think—and it's essential to differentiate the rancor that comes from just petty squabbling from the tension that comes from passion and desire. You want to eliminate the one, and tolerate, and maybe even stoke, the other.

It might seem like we had two separate missions—making arms and making a film—but really, they were the same cause. What I loved about Tim Freccia and Adrian is that they shared my passion for telling a story and my belief that it can truly make a difference. Focusing on one person with a help one, help many philosophy is not just the center of the Not Impossible Labs approach—it also happens to be the best way to tell a story. You can't overwhelm people by showing them the breadth of the devastation over here—or anywhere. But if you can make it easier for them to relate to one person, Daniel in this case, if you can touch them with his story, make them feel his heart, care about his plight, then you can bring them to the place where they can want to make a difference as well.

And that's how change happens: through a clear and simple, relatable story.

Focusing on the task at hand was helping me in a lot of ways. For one, it was keeping my mind off the approximately eight bazillion mosquito bites I'd acquired already. And off the fact that it had been a little less than four months from the time I first had dinner with Matt Keller, to this moment. So we got down on our hands and knees and sorted out the gear: This will be our camera box, these are the prosthetic boxes, here are our sleeping bags and some whiskey for Dr. Tom.

Hey, if I'd been out there in the middle of nowhere so long, I'd need a drink, wouldn't you?

◆

In fact, after we got our usual four hours of sleep, I needed a drink as soon as I woke up, because we learned that our flight had been canceled. No reason, no idea why—it just wasn't happening. Everybody else was taking it in stride—"Well, this is Africa, after all," Peter and

Tim kept saying—but I was frustrated as hell. I really wanted to get to Yida and get started. We talked about chartering a flight to Thar Jath, an airstrip at an oil exploration base, and driving from there to Yida, but we'd heard that the roads up there were in pretty bad shape. Even if they were passable, they went through some of the most heavily contested areas in the country, where the government of South Sudan, the army of the North, and one of the factions of the SPLA were having nearly daily skirmishes.

So we decided to just cool our jets and spent the day driving around Juba, taking some photos, doing some interviews, and saying hello to strangers. What I saw that day was really remarkable: how regardless of their circumstances and situation, people manage to be happy and to smile. Granted, in the capital city, people do have some infrastructure, some revenue, some ability to fulfill their basic needs; but they're still living in an impoverished, war-torn country. And yet people smile, they're cheerful, they wave and joke and laugh. It's almost like there's a need to be happy on a molecular level that supersedes your surroundings.

We got back to our hotel, to the pungent intense smell of burning horns tinged with a wisp of frankincense, to the legions of mosquitoes that give you the feeling of playing Russian roulette with a malaria gun, to the fact that our entire trip was stalled for no reason with no great assurance that we would in fact make it to Yida anytime soon, to our little foray into the police station for the crime of photographing a wheelbarrow. As much as I would like to say I had learned a lesson from the people of Juba, the delays were just grinding at me. I was getting more annoyingly intense by the minute.

Once again, Peter saved the day. He got wind of a Good Samaritan group that was flying some children from Juba to a small village and then continuing on to the refugee camp in Yida. We raced to the plane with all our gear and took our place among the children. They had all had cleft palate repair surgery the day before, so their little faces were all swollen and stitched up. They still had their medical bracelets on and were all passed out in their parents' arms or had their heads down in their parents' laps. And then this huge motley crew, this six-foot-six bald white guy and some old Obi-Wan Kenobi guy with a cane, and two war correspondent photographer types all squeezed in next to them.

And we were off to Yida.

And I had to keep reminding myself to breathe.

◆

When you've been to Tourist Africa, up around Morocco or down in South Africa, you think of the country as very green. As we flew away from Juba, the landscape was green and lush. But as we were approaching our landing strip in Yida, the landscape grew more and more brown. Here and there you'd see a pumpkin patch or something growing, but mostly it was brown dirt, brown buildings, brown everything. A rusty, barren place.

As the plane landed, I was startled to see two crashed planes on the side of the runway. No one had ever bothered to remove them—they just dragged them to the side of the runway and kept going about their business. And I'm not talking about some little Cessna—these were big, like DC-3s, and a huge bunch of kids was playing in and around them. When I got off the plane, the kids absolutely swarmed us—all wanting to get close to this big funny-looking bald white guy. It took a few minutes to extricate ourselves from that crowd and get to the Land Cruiser that was waiting for us.

We drove into the refugee camp, and nothing I'd read, nothing I'd seen, not even the video that Ken has shown me back in Juba, could have prepared me for this. It was a massive, sprawling, chaotic mess, spread as far as the eye could see. Nearly seventy thousand people, the size of a small city. Only, nothing like a city at all.

For miles, there were huts—and huts is giving them something, because they were more like raw dried straw tents, held together with rope and spit and what little prayers these people had left. The

Me with part of the welcoming committee on the landing strip in Yida.

scarcity of food, of clothing, of water, of medical attention was evident everywhere.

Most of the trees had been chopped down, which explained why the landscape looked so brown from the air. The area was barren and desolate; some of the little huts had just a tarp over them, which gave everything an even more disjointed feel, these acres and acres of brown huts, and here and there one of them sporting a bright blue or white tarp with a UN insignia on it. There were goats, dogs, all sorts of animals, like Noah's Ark had crashed, and the survivors had sought refuge here as well. There was no sanitation system whatsoever—just some deep holes dug in the ground here and there for water, and no organized waste system, just a few more shallow holes dug here and there for latrines. Someone told me that in the dry season, all of that filthy water evaporates and the waste dries and gets blown into the air, so you're basically breathing in feces all day long.

And this is supposed to be a place of refuge. This is better than the places these people had left. They'd all lost loved ones; some of them had lost their whole families, shot dead right in front of their eyes, raped, tortured. They'd all lived through unimaginable horrors.

And yet, once again, I was blown away by the joy I saw. Not by the disgusting nature of the camp, not by the smell, or by the horrendous conditions, or by the thought of how people could possibly live like this, how we as a world can tolerate people living in these conditions.

What blew me away was the joy.

A man with a homemade guitar—one of the many people in the camp I was stunned to find making a joyous noise.

I walked through the camp in a kind of a daze, and I saw people laughing and smiling and joking with each other, like it was a perfectly normal day in a perfectly normal town. By the side of the main road through the huts, a bunch of kids were playing with a soccer ball they'd found someplace. A few of them were kicking it around, and a bunch of others were chasing each other with a stick in their hand, around and around in circles, dodging and weaving like running backs, the way boys do. The way all boys do. I thought, if my boys were here, if I plopped Angus and Bo and Trace in the middle of this, once they got over the fact that they were separated from their normal lives and that they couldn't watch movies on the iPad, they would be doing exactly what these boys are doing. Try to tag me. I'm going to run that way. No, I was faking. I'm running this way. Ha, fooled you again. Can't touch this. I could do this all day.

And wafting over their heads were the sounds of chants and songs from their parents nearby: beautiful songs, in a rhythm that sounded a thousand years old, happy voices singing in harmony as though the universe were unfolding exactly as it was supposed to. And in that moment I felt the same way, as though I were doing exactly what I was supposed to do, too.

We walked a little farther and came upon a bustling, functioning marketplace. You can't imagine the cognitive dissonance of seeing a marketplace in a refugee camp—it's like coming across a shopping mall on the moon. But there, in the middle of this desolate, desperate place, people had opened little shops and were selling things, and somehow people had actual money and were buying them. Everything from pots and pans, to meat and barbecue, even cell phones. How the hell could someone be selling cell phones in a place like this? There isn't even any cell phone reception for miles. But there they were. I guess there will always and forever be trade. Someone told me that there had been a marketplace here before the camp, and the camp grew up around these shops, and the shops just stayed. There was even a little bar, with a cooler and some plastic chairs, and you could belly up to the bar and get a soda.

We were staying at the little compound of the Diocese of El Obeid. The compound consisted of five tents, two storage containers, and a ten-foot-high fence enclosing everything. We met Philippe, who runs the compound, a sincere and genuine guy from Cameroon who grew up in London. Philippe was an IT specialist, which came in incredibly handy later. We explained our mission to him, and told him how much we were hoping to find Daniel.

And he said, Oh, you want to meet Daniel? Is now a good time?

We were dumbstruck. My jaw actually physically dropped open.

Yes, we stammered. That would be a good thing.

Oh, he replied. No problem. Daniel is right over there.

I was nervous, as we walked over toward another little hut—a little like I felt when I first met Tempt, like a teenager going on a blind date. What would he think? Would he like me?

We entered the hut, and there, sitting with three other amputees, was the kid who started our whole mission, who got us all running around to 3-D printer companies, and to Johannesburg, and onto the plane to Yida—it felt like my whole universe was revolving around this young man. And now, here he was.

And he wouldn't look at us.

Daniel was very reclusive and very sad. He sat on the ground, the stumps of his arms pressed against his sides, his gaze fixed on a spot on the floor, like he was watching some tiny creature make its way through the dirt. It didn't seem like he would interact with us at all.

I focused my attention on the other amputees gathered in the hut, all the while keeping Daniel in my peripheral vision. I took out a marker and drew a Mickey Mouse on the side of my hand, the way you do so that your index finger is the upper lip and your thumb is the lower lip so you can make him talk, and in my best falsetto started saying hello to them in Mickey Mouse talk. Daniel's brother, Shaki, sitting next to him, started cracking up. Daniel tried to stifle a little smile, but I knew I'd at least gotten his attention. He watched for a minute or two and then he turned away again.

I thought of what Daniel had told a reporter after the bombing. "Without hands, I can't do anything. I can't even fight. I'm going to make such hard work for my family in the future. If I could have died, I would have."

I looked down at this young boy and tried to imagine having so little hope at so young an age. I could almost hear the sound of my own heart breaking.

We tried to interview him, through an interpreter, but he was monosyllabic in his answers. We decided to wait and come back later.

Philippe told me a little later that Daniel had been to Uganda twice to get fitted for prosthetics that were just aesthetic, not functional, and were very uncomfortable, so when he returned he'd just thrown them on the ground and said, I can't wear this. And I thought, oh, man. This is gonna be hard. Those were full-on prosthetic companies, not some stubborn dude from Venice Beach with a 3-D printer. But I was encouraged, too, because our arms weren't just for looks. They work. They're a little crude, but you can pick stuff up, you can do stuff. I was sure that once Daniel saw what we were up to, he would get excited.

I hoped so, anyway. Our plan was to get Daniel to Gidel, where the hospital is, where Dr. Tom Catena is, where I could really set up my equipment and get the hand printed and show him how it would work, and then things would be much better.

But life was busy making other plans.

◆

That very afternoon, we had everything ready to go to Gidel, up in the Nuba Mountains, the contested area that was being controlled by the SPLA-N. Daniel and four other amputees were all loaded in the truck, along with all our gear. We were just about to get on the road, when a very imposing plain-clothed security guard, a very big, very muscular guy in a perfectly pressed clean tan shirt and pants with a crease in the front you could shave with, walks up and in perfect English quite calmly tells us, "I'm sorry, but for security reasons you're not going to be able to go."

Mister Producer Guy kicked in, and I was all, Hey, no, we gotta go, man. Peter, somebody, tell this guy, we gotta get on the road, no kidding. But Mister Security Guy was a lot more determined than Mister Producer Guy. Actually, his name was Joshua, and later he became a friend of ours, but right at the moment, he was a boulder in the road that couldn't be moved. We had no idea why we were being stopped. Joshua calmly explained that the ceasefire had ended, so this was now no longer a tense area teetering on war—this was an active war zone. I couldn't come up with an argument as strong as the words "active war zone." So we were stuck.

It was devastating, to be sitting in the back of a truck with four kids who were all missing limbs, to have spent months arranging this impossible mission, and to have come so far, and then to be told, well, no, it ends here.

That critical voice inside—the one that says, See, you can't do it, I don't know why you thought you could—began to kick in. The voice we've all heard, the one that stops us from trying, the one that says, just accept your failure. It'll be so much easier if you just accept defeat.

And then that other voice kicked in.

The voice that says, Screw that.

We decided right there on the spot: We are here in Yida. The printers are here in Yida. Daniel is here in Yida. If we can't make it to Gidel, then we can't make it to Gidel. Fine.

We'll set up our own prosthetics lab right here in Yida.

It was going to be hard, we were quite aware.

Hard.

But not impossible.

CHAPTER 13

What If Nothing Is Impossible?

Which would you rather have screw you up totally: the heat or the insects? That was the choice we faced when we tried to make a hand for Daniel in Yida.

We had transferred our operation to a larger compound, run by the non-governmental organization that was watching out for us; the officials of the group asked me not to name them, because they feel that staying anonymous allows them to help people without getting involved in the political situation. I wish I could tell you more about them. They're humble, gracious, remarkable people.

Compared to the DOE compound, this one was immense. To the left of the entrance were parked the ATVs and Land Cruisers that the volunteers used to get around the camp; to the right, the tents where they lived. Tim was bunking with me, and I would learn soon enough that the man can snore louder than anyone I'd ever known.

Farther in front, there was a big round hut that served as a gathering place for meals and meetings and group activities, and a smaller tent that served as a makeshift commissary. Behind them was a kitchen, a generator shack, and a fairly large toolshed, which would become my entire world for the next seven days. The shed was about the size of a one-car garage with no windows. A second open shed was attached to it, with a tarp for a roof. Next to them was a third, smaller, open structure with a metal roof, which I set up as my printing station.

The next day, Daniel and his younger brother, Shaki, walked over right on time—we gave them breakfast, so they were always on time. It was kind of amazing to learn of how Shaki had been taking care of Daniel—feeding him, dressing him, wiping him, doing everything for him—without complaint, without fuss, as though it were the most normal thing in the world. It was even more astounding when I found out that although they called each other "brothers," they weren't, actually. In their culture, I learned, it's pretty common to call someone brother or uncle, even when you are distantly related; Daniel's dad was Shaki's dad's second cousin, or something like that. To see Shaki caring for Daniel was, for me, a lesson in true, unconditional love. It was pretty humbling.

After breakfast, they settled in for what I'd warned them would be a long day. Daniel had more patience than any fourteen-year-old boy I'd ever met. Over the next few days, he would sit for hours on end, just watching me work. I can't imagine my own kids doing that for more than ten minutes.

But kids are more the same than they are different, I have to say. We'd brought some tablets with us to drive the 3-D printers; We gave them to Daniel and Shaki to use while we were getting things set up. We had loaded them up with some video games, and although the boys had probably never seen a tablet or a video game in their lives, it took them about no seconds to get totally into it. It was a bit surreal, seeing Daniel using the stumps of his arms as deftly as other kids use their thumbs and forefingers to race cars on the screen. He was blasting aliens and tossing angry birds around like any suburban kid in America, only doing it in the midst of such primitive surroundings, such bleak devastation.

But there we were. Daniel and Shaki, playing their video games, while I labored nearby, trying to make Daniel a new hand. Trying and failing and cursing, I should say.

Occasionally, I would call Daniel over so I could adjust the arm fittings or test some part of the arm. He would be in the middle of a

Me with Shaki and Daniel. Kids are kids, wherever you go.

video game, and would do what any fourteen-year-old does when an adult calls them away from a video game. He would ignore me. I'd say, "Daniel! Come on. Come over here." And he would regretfully relinquish control of the video game to Shaki, who would snatch it from him; and then Daniel would drag himself over to me, sighing and letting out a low moan, to make sure I knew he was not happy that he had had to give up what was surely his high score of the day.

As I've said, kids everywhere are more the same than they are different.

The 3-D printers just didn't want to work in that 100-degree heat. The shed was so blasted hot that the filament kept melting onto itself on the spool and wouldn't feed through the extruder.

We put two oscillating fans on the printers, which seemed to work at first, But it was so dusty that the fans blew a lot of dirt into the motors, so they clogged up and stopped working, and we had to take them apart and fix them. We finally gave up and decided to print at night, when it was cooler. It was late by the time I finally got everything working properly. I stuck around for the first hour of night printing, and all seemed to be going swimmingly. Exhausted, I locked up with the padlock the NGO had given me, donned my head lamp, and headed off to find my tent and my foghorn of a tent mate.

The next morning, I woke up and ran excitedly to the shed to see if we had gotten a first print off. But when I unlocked the shed, much to my dismay I discovered that not only had we *not* gotten a print off successfully, but I was going to have to spend the morning extracting the carcasses of these prehistoric-sized moths from the printer motors. We had not taken into account the fact that there were so many more bugs at night. The light that the printer gave off attracted these creatures, and they had jammed themselves into the printer motors in some sort of crazed kamikaze bug mission.

So there was our choice: Deal with the computer bugs in the system by day or deal with actual bugs clogging up the system by night. It was making me crazy.

But somehow, after about a day of trying, we managed to print a hand for Daniel.

Or all the pieces of a hand, anyway. I was pretending not to be terrified that, for only the second time in my life—and the first time completely unsupervised—I was going to try to assemble a full arm and hand and fit it on an actual person in a way that would actually allow him to do something; in this case, our first and primary goal was for him to feed himself.

Daniel, in some ways, has the face of an old man; he has a tiredness in his eyes, a world-weary long stare, almost as though he had sunk deep inside himself and saw no good reason to climb back out. And besides, I was interrupting his video-game time. He showed little emotion during the process of fitting him. His left arm was amputated just below the elbow, so that was the arm we'd decided to work with. I had printed a small plastic sleeve to go above the elbow and a longer section to attach to the stump of his arm, and I was working on the metal strings that would attach from the hinge between the two, down to the hand itself. My handy-dandy Dremel had run out of juice and we couldn't rig it to take a charge—it was a 110-volt device, and we couldn't adapt it to the local current—so I was going to have to file the ends of the attachments by hand, a long, slow, painful, incredibly dull process.

Doing dull work in the hot sun is about as tedious as it gets, but Daniel sat and watched, patiently, occasionally chatting with his little brother in Arabic, drifting off to play video games or kick the soccer ball around in the dirt outside the shed. The only rise I got out of him was when I went to heat some water over a charcoal fire to form the orthoplastic, and on the way back cracked my forehead into the metal overhang of the structure we were using as a printing station, and gave myself a giant cut that would be my insignia for the rest of the trip. Daniel and his brother thought that was very, very funny. As I said, kids are more the same than they are different.

After a couple of hours, I finally had the hard part done—the hand assembly, with the wires running down from it, so that when you pull the wires, the fingers make a grasping motion toward the palm, and when you release them, they spring back open.

Kind of like you're waving hello.

Our translator went missing, but Daniel and I managed to communicate okay. "Close your eyes," I told him, and waved my hand over my eyes, and he got the point, and closed them. I swear that a little smile was curling the corner of his lips. I brought the hand in front of him and told him to open his eyes.

Then I made it wave at him.

And that tiny smile turned into a great big teenage boy grin, the kind that any father of boys knows and loves and lives for; the kind that anyone seeing a skinny, malnourished, dirty, disheveled, beautiful young man who had lost his arms to a senseless, senseless war would take one look at and say, I am so lucky to be here, in this moment, to witness this tiny bit of joy amid all this sorrow.

It was November 11, 2013—exactly four months, to the day, that I had the fateful dinner in Venice Beach that started me on this path. And look where my journey had taken me.

This is what I meant when I said that doing things for others is an ultimately selfish act, and that there's nothing wrong with that. This moment gave me—me—such great, great pleasure.

What gives you pleasure? Your family, your job, your movies, your TV shows? Food, drink, drugs, boats, cars, vacations, sailing, skiing, sex? I'll give you all of those, and I'll raise you one armless boy, seeing his new hand wave at him for the first time, and grinning at you with a grin so big that his bright white teeth shine like diamonds in the noonday sun.

◆

That joy turned back to tedium, as I drilled holes to screw the long arm extension that would fit on the end of Daniel's stump onto the hinge that attached it to the smaller part that would fit his forearm. Fortunately the drill I'd brought took a charge, so at least I didn't have to do this part by hand. I rubbed some baby powder onto the end of Daniel's stump, so that the arm wouldn't irritate him, and after some adjustments, worked the two pieces on so that they were fairly snug but not too tight.

I asked Daniel to extend his arm forward, so that the structure was sticking straight out, and I told him to raise it—*up* was a word he knew. I was hoping he could bend his stump below the elbow, the way you'd raise your own forearm while keeping your upper arm steady. I gotta tell you, as much as I knew it was going to work, I held my breath.

And up it went. And down. And up. And down.

It worked!

Shaki came over to see his big brother's new arm.

And Daniel did what any good teenage boy would do to his brother.

He knocked him in the head with it playfully and both of them collapsed in laughter.

I started working much faster now—funny how much easier this was, just having done it once before—and by early that afternoon, Daniel's hand was attached.

It was almost time for lunch. I melted a little piece of the orthoplastic onto the palm of the hand, so it made a little slot that a spoon could fit into. It took a little adjusting to get the angle just right, so that Daniel could bring it to his mouth. I made some adjustments to the arm and the angle of the spoon, and we got ready. I was so excited, tears started to well up in my eyes. But I held them back.

Now's not the time for tears, I thought.

Now it's showtime.

Or, more specifically: It's lunchtime.

◆

We went over to the area where we usually ate and a whole group had gathered for lunch—Philippe, and some of my team, and some of Philippe's colleagues from the wonderful and generous NGO. Someone brought Daniel a bowl of stew, a mixture of bread and goat and some pieces of pumpkin, and set it down in front of him.

The lunch tent was normally a noisy, bustling place, everyone jabbering away at once, plates clattering and clanging all around you—but as Daniel lowered his spoon toward the bowl, the area became silent.

And he lifted the spoon to his lips, and took a bite, and looked up to the crowd, beaming.

And it was like an eruption: all around him, people were gasping, clapping, putting their hands to their mouths; a big black woman and a skinny white guy grabbed each other and started hugging. People who had watched me warily for days, wondering what I was up to, wondering if I was actually going to do what I said that

I was going to do, were looking at me and laughing as if to say, well done, man, well done.

Daniel was feeding himself, sloppily and hungrily, just like any other teenage boy. Oddly, in that moment, I flashed on my own boys again and how I wanted them to meet Daniel. It was almost like he had become part of the family.

It was an incredible moment, for all of us. This kid who had gone to Uganda and been fitted for prosthetics, only to toss them on the ground because they were uncomfortable and useless— suddenly, he's responding, he's smiling, he's—he's oh my lord feeding himself. Somebody had baked a little stash of brownies, and one of the guys from the NGO brought them over. Daniel had never tasted chocolate before. And if you think the sight of a kid seeing his own hand wave to him for the first time would warm your heart, imagine the sight of that kid feeding himself, for the first time, a chocolate brownie.

Daniel, of course, ate three.

◆

For the first time since the bombing, Daniel feeds himself.

We finally learned why we had been stopped from going to Gidel: it wasn't just that it had become an active war zone. It was also because of Peter. Among the many hats Peter wears, he is a journalist, and journalists are the one group that is distrusted more than any other in the Sudan. Even though we all had press passes, Peter was the one who was well known in the area, and he figured someone had it in for him; so, rather than try to figure out who or exactly why, he agreed, begrudgingly, not to come along. Once he withdrew from the excursion to Gidel, the powers that be somehow decided that the rest of us could go. His decision turned out to be a blessing in more ways than one, because he came down with a horrific case of malaria, and there's no way he could have survived the eleven-hour Land Cruiser ride anyway.

The night before we left Yida for Gidel, I finally took a minute to catch my breath. I walked around the storeroom, listening to the sounds—the constant drone of the generators coming from the NGO camp, the chirping of crickets and some other odd bugs I'd never heard before, calling to each other through the dark. I'd given the printers the night off—I still hadn't gotten the computers and the printers to make nice with each other regularly and consistently, so it's amazing that we were able to accomplish what we did.

Earlier that afternoon, we had gone to visit Daniel's hut on the outskirts of the refugee camp, so we had to drive a ways. It cracked us up on the drive when we came to a fork in the road and Daniel, without a moment's hesitation, pointed and said, in perfect English, "That way," because those were the first English words he'd spoken—damn near the only words he'd spoken at all—since we met him. It's like that moment in *One Flew Over the Cuckoo's Nest* when McMurphy gives the big Indian guy a stick of gum—the guy's supposed to be mute but he smiles and says, "Mmmm. Juicy Fruit," and the two of them grin at each other like they've just shared the biggest secret in the universe. And in a way, Daniel and I had shared a big secret—we'd both learned something we never knew before, anyway—and we'd broken some kind of barrier, formed some kind of bond, and it was all wrapped up in those two simple words.

That way.

So we drove that way, to the place where the road ends, and got out and started walking through a maze of dirt paths through a thousand thatched huts with Daniel and Shaki leading the way. We were impressed that they could even find their way: we'd walk and turn and walk some more, and hit a fork and another fork and turn left and right and left again; and wherever we went, children were running up to us and yelling, "Khawaja! Khawaja!"—Juba Arabic for "white person"—but we finally got to an area where there were two huts attached to each other by a small covered area. One of those was Daniel and Shaki's hut. The other belonged to Daniel's uncle and aunt, and we stopped there first. It was immaculately clean—they had clearly swept the dirt floor very carefully, so it seemed as manicured as the sand trap at a golf course.

We sat and talked with them for a while, but our translator was a kid who was just learning English, so the conversation was pretty short. But we managed to let them know what we were doing, and they were grateful and gracious. Then we walked over to Daniel and Shaki's tiny hut, with a thatched roof and dirt floors, and three little nylon bed-type devices—basically four sticks tied together for legs and four crossbeams at the top, and some nylon string run between them, and a dirty, nasty little blanket on top. Daniel and Shaki lived there with one other boy—no adults; Daniel's father, from what I gathered, was fighting in the war, and his mother was in Khartoum. I don't know where Shaki's parents were. So there's just these three boys, crammed in one little room, and it looked like any messy boys' room—stuff was strewn all about, and in one corner were all their earthly possessions, pots and pans and some plastic cups and utensils, little things like that. The boys didn't have a single thing they wanted to bring with them to Gidel. We just hung around for a while, and then we left.

A massive crowd had gathered to see us, the Khawaja and the Magic Hand. Some girls had made some spinning devices out of branches that were just like the toys we played with as kids—tubes that would make a low musical note when you spun them around your head—and the girls were spinning them and somehow managing to make a kind of music. A mother was holding a little one-year-old and pointing to make her look at me, and the child took one look at the big bald white guy and started screaming like she had seen a ghost.

Which, apparently, was the funniest thing that had happened all day, because the crowd erupted in laughter, and the laughter blended in with the music from the girls with their spinning branches, and that was the soundtrack of our moment. We had brought Daniel into the world of Robohands, and now Daniel had brought us into his world.

Just for laughs.

◆

That night, as I packed up the printers for the next day's trip, I reflected on the day's events, and I thought how nice it would be when we got to Gidel, to the hospital—a primitive hospital to be sure, but compared to what we've been trying to work with, I thought, it'll be like going to Johns Hopkins. And to have other folks there to help me out—folks who know a lot more about all this stuff than I do—would be a blessing.

But then I stopped, and thought, No. *This* was the blessing.

The whole rigmarole—the fact that everyone else on the technical side of this operation dropped out or wasn't able to come, the fact that I had to learn to make hands all on my own, the fact that it was so hard to get to Yida, the fact that we were stopped from going to Gidel when we were supposed to—all of it, suddenly, felt like some grand design. A huge bargain with the Big Guy. A big blessing.

Because if any one of those things hadn't happened—if all those dominoes hadn't fallen—then I never would have had to face this challenge. I never would have been forced to do something that I quite secretly thought was impossible, and I never would have learned how to get past that.

I had launched the Not Impossible site several months earlier—but this was the night, this was the moment, that I became a true believer.

Because if a guy like me can make an arm for an amputee at the end of the earth—then clearly, nothing is impossible. If you take anything at all from this book, I hope you take that: If this guy Mick can accomplish what he accomplished, what could I do if I set my mind to it?

I promise you, if you take the time to consider it, you'll find ways to amaze yourself. And maybe, just maybe, find a path to walk that you've never walked before. It may be a kind of a maze, there may be a lot of twists and turns—but trust me. It's worth it because of what you find at the end.

◆

Gidel is tucked up in the mountains, about a ten-hour, brutal truck ride from Yida. We were bouncing along in the back of the truck, passing a lot of people walking in both directions. The ones walking toward the camp were empty-handed; the ones walking the other way were carrying bags of food. I was about to ask someone about this strange migration when I saw Daniel lean over to say something to Shaki. I was curious so I asked our translator what he said. He told me, "Daniel said, 'Shaki, I just saw your mother.'" And they were both so nonchalant about it, like it was the most natural thing in the world, but I was stunned. I flashed on that line in Camus's *The Stranger*, when the main character says, "Mother died today. Or maybe yesterday; I can't be sure." There was something so strangely unaffected about it, about that blasé reaction to something that enormous. Again, I realized how much I couldn't understand unless

I'd lived through what these boys had been through. Nothing goes by normal rules after that.

The translator told me that most of the people on the road live up in the Nuba Mountains, but they check themselves into the refugee camp and get a ration card so they can collect food every fifteen days. It's a three-day walk from their homes to the camp. Women with babies, four- or five-year-old kids, elderly men—all trek three days down and three days back for food. Occasionally someone went by on a motorcycle, but fuel was expensive and rare, so mostly it was men and women and young children, and donkeys carrying bags of sorghum. I thought of how my kids would ask, "Daddy, up, up," and make me carry them after fifteen minutes of walking, and these kids by the side of the road had been walking for days and days and days.

Hearing Daniel be so nonchalant about Shaki seeing his mother, I realized that it might not occur to him to point out to us where he grew up. So I asked Daniel, "Are we going near the place where you got your arms blown off?" And Daniel looked around, and said, quite matter-of-factly, "Yes." And he pointed off toward about two o'clock from where we were driving. We needed to ride a little while longer, and then Daniel pointed to a spot just off the road, and we pulled over. The crew started unloading their camera gear off the truck; they wanted to get some shots of Daniel at the place where this strange journey began. A giant grasshopper landed on Daniel's upper arm, but he didn't take any notice of it. I asked him if it would be okay to go visit the bombing site. I felt a little uncomfortable about it; but again, for a kid who's been through what he's been through, it was like asking if he minded when that grasshopper landed on his arm. Daniel just shrugged and nodded okay.

We walked toward a little group of tukuls—cone-shaped mud huts—where Daniel had lived before the accident. The area seemed fairly deserted, but as we got near the house where Daniel had lived, a woman came out and gave him a big hug; Daniel introduced her as his aunt and we talked a bit. She saw the arm that he was wearing and couldn't believe her eyes. The translator introduced us, and I gotta say, while you don't go into something like this for the thank-yous, no one has ever expressed more gratitude to me for anything in my life than this woman did for her nephew's new arm.

She joined us as we walked on to find the place where the accident occurred. I was nervous; this was the place where this boy's life was changed irrevocably and forever, and I wondered if I had a made a cruel mistake.

Daniel looked around and finally pointed and said, "This is it." And he just stared, quietly, for a moment, and I could see that he was trying to process everything.

I asked him, "Daniel, how are you feeling right now?"

He looked over at me and shrugged and grunted, as always. Then he mumbled something, and the translator told me he'd said, "You always ask me how I feel."

"I know," I said. "So how are you feeling right now?"

I didn't really expect an answer, because he never answers that question. But this time, he looked slowly around, his eyes squinting a little, as if he were, for the first time, seeing into his own past, seeing a time before the bombs, a time when he had arms and a family and some semblance of a normal life.

"I am angry," he said, finally. "I am angry that all this took place."

It was probably the longest sentence he'd ever spoken to me. He looked at me. What could I say? I was speechless. We stood and stared at the scene of the crime. There was nothing more to say. Just then, Daniel broke out in a little laugh—that Nuba reaction I'd learned to expect. What else can you do? You look, you process, you laugh. You move on.

We walked back to the house in the village. A man with enormous hands, who had been working in a field nearby, came walking up; he turned out to be Daniel's uncle. Another aunt showed up as well, and when she saw Daniel, she stopped for a second and then came running up to him, crying hysterically, and sweeping him up in her arms. Daniel was happy, but squirmed a bit, showing a hint of that awkwardness any teenage boy shows at a family reunion when his aunt starts pinching his cheeks.

We stood and talked with them for more than an hour as other people from the village showed up, more aunts and uncles and friends. I was struck by the casual attitude these people had about living in a war zone. Many people had fled to camps like Yida, but I hadn't realized how many had stayed. I asked about the bombings, if they were still going on, and they told me that they were. But the villagers didn't seem particularly concerned about them—they regarded the bombings almost as though they were nothing more than bad weather. They didn't even seem to know why the war was happening—who the president was or which side was bombing them—and didn't seem to particularly care. They just went about their business, feeding themselves, keeping life and limb together, and trying not to stand where the bomb lands.

I thought about that email Richard Van As had sent me, telling me I was crazy to come here. Well, maybe I am crazy. But if this is what comes of crazy, then maybe crazy isn't such a bad thing.

Daniel and his aunt, on the day he returned to the bomb site for the first time since the accident.

Eventually, it came time to go. I put my arm around Daniel's shoulder, and we started trudging back to the truck; but as we did, he took one more look over his shoulder, at all the folks watching him go, and then he looked up at me. He didn't say anything, but I could feel his shoulders relax, I could feel that the tension that was always present with him had eased, just a bit. I allowed myself to believe that something had clicked in him. That maybe, just maybe, he had decided that it was okay, after all, to be alive.

◆

Around midnight, after what seemed like a million hours on rough, bumpy roads, we came into Gidel and pulled up to a long, low, L-shaped structure nestled among a few trees. A handpainted sign in English and Arabic announced that we were at the Mother of Mercy Hospital, Diocese of El Obeid. It was a thrill for me to meet Dr. Tom Catena—at this point he had become like a rock star to me. Like meeting a guru. He was gracious and humble; yet he had an intensity and conviction about him. It was strange for me, in this place, to be face-to-face with another tall bald white guy. Dr. Tom was thin; he wore small, round, wire-framed glasses, green scrubs; a stethoscope dangled from his neck. The hospital had the simple green walls and small cots with green blankets I'd seen in the video. It was full of amputees with bandaged arms, and many other patients as well, their faces sunken and sad.

There were eight of us and only three spare beds, so we all bunked together and crashed on floors wherever we could—except we gave Tim the Snoring Monster his own room.

The next morning, Dr. Tom showed us around the hospital. And what an operation it was. The hospital had been set up to accommodate two hundred beds, but after the war broke out, the injured kept coming. On the walls above the beds were little paper signs numbering up to 400. There were patients in the hallways and under makeshift tarps and lean-tos in the courtyard. Patients' families slept in

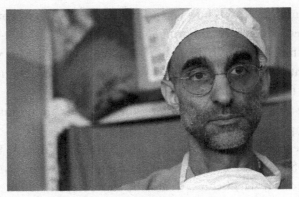

The incredible Doctor Tom Catena, at his hospital in Gidel.

the courtyard on mats on top of the dirt. It was a little like being in a MASH unit, only ten times worse. Everything felt urgent, everyone needed attention.

Dr. Tom had chosen a group of young local men for us to train to make the arm, and they joined us as we toured the facility. We set up our equipment in a room adjacent to the hospital office and got ready to make some arms.

The room was crowded—in addition to the men whom I was going to train, it seemed like everyone in the village had crowded in to see these miracle machines. A lot of these folks had never seen a computer before, let alone a printer, let alone a 3-D printer. Because the ceasefire had ended, and because our trip had been delayed, the fourteen days we'd planned to spend in Gidel had turned into five. There was so little time and so much to do. Occasionally throughout the day, I would have to ask people to leave because it would get so crowded. One of the villagers, a young man named Achmed, always hung in the wings whenever everyone was asked to leave. Achmed was a happy but persistent fellow, with a quiet but forceful personality.

I started the class with the absolute basics—this is a drill, this is how you load the drill. This is filament, this is how you load the filament into the printer. This is how you call up the 3-D files on the computer. This is how you print a comb; this is how you print a bracelet. This is how you print an arm.

Achmed was still there, but I figured someone who was that motivated to help just might be useful. And sure enough, he turned out to be one of the best arm-makers we had.

Just goes to show you, asking forgiveness is always easier than asking permission.

We worked through the day, using Daniel as a model. That first day, a Saturday, I was really just teaching them the basics. Sunday was a down day, because that's the day everyone either went to church or to see family members who lived out of town. Monday was our first real day, and slowly but surely, they started understanding how to make a hand. They had to take on so much, and they learned so much in such a short amount of time: heating water over charcoal to soften the molding plastic, using tools they'd never seen before. One of the men had never held a drill before, and when he turned it on, it startled him so that he dropped it, and all the men laughed. Working on computers when they'd never touched a computer before. And, of course, the computers came loaded with some American music; these men had no access to music, and they played the songs over and over and over until I screamed. I mean, there's just so much Kesha a man can take.

But little by little, it was happening. People who had never used a computer before learned to print a hand on a 3-D printer.

It kind of takes your breath away.

◆

The next day, I was teaching the Robohand class again, and feeling pretty great, when Dr. Tom came barging in. "A ten-year-old boy was just admitted who had his arm blown off by a bomber," he said.

The boy had been brought in by his uncle, who had related the terrible tale: They'd been out in the field the day before, when the MiGs came. The bombs killed the boy's seven- and eight-year-old

Daniel and me at the computer. Daniel is 3-D printing for the first time.

brothers, and the boy's left arm was blown to pieces. The arm was swaddled in some kind of clothing, soaked and caked with blood, and would clearly need to be amputated. They had driven all night, but their car had broken down, and they had to sleep by the side of the road. They'd made the rest of the trip to the hospital this morning.

I was overcome with shock, with dismay, with horror, with sadness.

And resolve.

Dr. Tom ran off to begin the amputation procedure, and as I watched him leave, I thought, if I can make a tenth of the contribution this man is making—a hundredth, a thousandth—then all of this will have been worthwhile. It would be many months before that boy would be able to be fitted for an arm, but I was resolved that he would get one. And these young men in the class would make it for him—only when they did, I wouldn't be here to help them. They were going to have to do it all on their own.

So I put everything out of my mind, except for one thought, which I shared with my students.

"Back to class, everyone," I said. "Let's make some arms."

◆

By that Wednesday, after a million problems and a million questions and a million mistakes and false starts, they had actually done it. They had made a new hand for Daniel.

Let me say that again:

THEY, my class who had never seen a 3-D printer before, had made a new hand for Daniel.

We had talked so long about the idea, give a man a fish and he eats today, teach a man to fish and he feeds himself. And we had taught these young men to print hands. The implications of that—not for Daniel alone, but for who knows how many other amputees in this very hospital—were staggering. Our stated goal had been to come here and make a hand for Daniel—help one—but our hope, of course, was that the project would find a way to carry on, day after day, arm after arm, long after we'd left. Help many.

And now, with this one Robohand completed, that goal was actually in sight.

They'd made a good hand, too—even better than the one I'd jerry-rigged back in Yida. At the end of the day, Daniel was finally able to try it on, and even though everyone was excited, we were all in a pissy mood, too. It was hot, we were tired, the machines had been acting up as usual. I had refused to let everyone take their usual three tea breaks a day. Everyone was just crabby.

Daniel was sitting at a table, testing out the arm, when Dr. Tom walked in. I decided to ignore Daniel's crummy mood. There was a rolled-up Ace bandage on the table, and I told Daniel to pick it up and pass it to Dr. Tom.

And Daniel leaned forward and moved the arm—and for the first time was able to get this new arm and hand to grab something. He reached down, and the hand clenched the Ace bandage, and slowly, slowly, he picked it up.

And reared back.

And threw a perfect bullet pass, straight to Dr. Tom's solar plexus.

Dr. Tom was an all-Ivy nose guard at Brown University, inducted into the Ivy League Hall of Fame—but I don't think the cheers at Brown Stadium were ever as loud as the roar that went up in that room, when Daniel completed that pass to Dr. Tom.

It was a moment of complete and utter joy. Daniel's smile was a mile wide. We all went out for a pass from Daniel—he completed almost every one. (I dropped mine. My hands aren't as quick as they used to be.)

The passing record, for the day, for Daniel: six for seven.

The record, for the day, for Project Daniel: a huge, huge touchdown.

◆

It was my last night in Gidel. I had found out that the ten-year-old boy who'd been admitted a few days earlier after his arm was blown off had had the arm amputated above the elbow. My heart sank once again, because right now we could only make arms that work for kids whose elbow joints survived the bombings. And in that very moment, I made myself another promise: a promise that I'd come back here again, and that the next time, we'd have figured out how to make a hand for a kid whose arm was amputated above the elbow.

I was on my way to dinner, and as I walked I looked off into the distance, the sun hanging low in the sky. The next trip, I thought. I got that done on the next trip.

It's in the future, but I've already started thinking of it in the past tense. Like it's a done deal. Like it's already happened. Because in my mind, it has.

◆

I left Gidel with a flurry of mixed emotions. As the Toyota Land Cruiser barreled along the rutted roads, I got a chance to look around. Everything seemed so beautiful: the people were beautiful, the landscape was beautiful. Sand-colored buildings with doors painted brilliant blues and greens were beautiful. The hugs I got when I left Gidel were beautiful. The cleaning lady who wanted to thank us and gave us a bucket of potatoes and peppers and herbs was beautiful. White teeth against black skin are beautiful, especially when they are on the face of a young boy who just a short time ago had been wishing he had been left for dead, and was now flinging Ace bandages at anyone in sight. It had been a whirlwind trip: I wished to God I'd been able to do more. Give more money, spend more time, teach more people, make more arms.

When I had said good-bye to him, Daniel hugged me like I had never been hugged before. His little stumps pulled me in and pressed into my back. I almost cried, because just days ago he had been a forlorn, recluse of a boy and he had opened himself up to me. I felt so sad as I was driving away, filled with a fear that I might never see him again, filled with a quiet resolve that I had to. But Africa is an unpredictable place, and I did not take our parting lightly. I miss him and Shaki dearly. I sometimes go weeks without hearing from Dr. Tom about how they are doing, and in the space of time between those reports, I hope and pray that they are okay.

Earlier that morning, as I had several times in Gidel, I went to Mass with Dr. Tom. My dad went to Mass every day, and when I got a little older I used to go with him; so going through this little morning ritual with Dr. Tom was a nice touchstone for me. We'd walk out of the hospital when it was still pitch black, through a riverbed and across a gully to a sweet, simple chapel. There would be eight or ten other people waiting, and the priest would come in and conduct a short service in English. It was nostalgic for me, bringing me back to a time in my life when I was very connected to my dad, but I also enjoy getting up before everyone else and having the world to myself, before the craziness and business begin, a time to reflect. More specifically, what brought me to the chapel was the belief that there is an entity or a power greater than myself. Whatever your religion, whatever name you give to that power, that belief fills you with a sense of humility, of wanting to strive to be better, of gratitude for what you have. It's wonderful, for me, to start my day with those feelings, because it gives me the chance to infuse the rest of my day with that humility, and gratitude, and hope.

After Mass we returned to the hospital, where the pace of the day picked up pretty quickly as we got ready to depart. The ceasefire, which was in place for some of our visit, had ended, and a truckload of wounded soldiers had pulled up to the hospital just before we left, so it's probably good that we got out when we did. We were stopped at a lot of checkpoints, and while we waited to see if they'd let us through, we could hear gunshots and explosions in the distance.

Joshua, our guide from the SPLA, had to stop and press the flesh and bargain at every checkpoint. At about our sixth checkpoint, I saw two soldiers, sitting and having a smoke under a big fat Tabaldi tree, placidly watching the chickens walking past them, seeming so calm, and yet within moments, they could be facing incredible danger, maybe even death.

I didn't want to think that we might be facing the same. I tried to keep that thought out of my mind, but at every checkpoint, someone wanted to get in the car with us, because they saw us as a way out—and you could see, in their eyes, the hope and the desperation, and you knew this was no idle hitchhiker, this was someone who was in fear for his own life. So as many as could fit, we let ride.

We put the pedal to the metal, trying to make it into South Sudan before the border closed at 6:00 p.m., but with all our riders, it was slow going. At one point, there were two people on top of the car, three in the front seat, eight in the back. We spent the night with Philippe back at the Diocese camp in Yida, and the next morning caught our plane to Juba. When we finally took off, something let loose in me. I felt a rush of emotions I'd been holding back throughout the trip in order to stay focused and do what needed to be done. I felt overwhelmed, but not by the sadness, the pain, of having seen such unimaginable human suffering—but by the feeling of positivity at all I had experienced. The sense of believing in the human spirit, believing in the capability of people to change, believing in their intelligence, in their ability to persevere in spite of all the challenges.

I believe in technology. I believe that technology for the good of humanity can be attained and that people can learn to use anything if there is some inherent good imbedded in it. I believe that anybody given the incentive to do good for the world will most likely strive for that.

I felt proud that I had changed a few people's lives. But I was honored and privileged to think of how much they had changed mine. Because I knew that when I got back to America, nothing was ever going to be the same.

I made a promise not to be a pain in the ass to my kids—not to see them in their world of first-world privilege and whine, "Eat your vegetables! Don't you know children are starving in Africa?" Because this was not what the trip was about.

It was not about learning just to appreciate what we have. It was about learning to appreciate all that we are capable of doing.

And I couldn't wait to find out what that would be.

CHAPTER 14

What Gets You Out of Bed?

I wasn't on the last plane out of Sudan. But it was pretty close.

I came back on the Monday before Thanksgiving. A few weeks later, all hell broke loose. The conflicts in Sudan started back up with horrible violence. The opposing tribes in South Sudan, the Dinka and the Nuer, had formed an uneasy alliance in their struggle against Omar al-Bashir and the government of Sudan in Khartoum. But ever since South Sudan gained independence in 2011, the conflicts between those tribes had increased, and on December 15 erupted again into civil war. Thousands were killed in a matter of days.

Within weeks, more than one hundred thousand people were fleeing South Sudan. But while the civil war raged in the south, President Bashir continued bombing rebels in the border areas. In fact, it increased: Bashir's government took this moment, while the world's eyes were on the south, to intensify the bombing of the rebels in the contested areas. The UN was caught quite literally in the crossfire and couldn't protect its own people, let alone the refugees in Yida. All aid workers in Yida were evacuated.

I was following these developments from the comfort of my nice cozy home in Venice Beach, surrounded by my wife and kids. During the day, we had returned to a nice, normal life.

At night, I was having nightmares.

I dreamed of Daniel; I don't remember the details of those dreams, only that they were filled with dread. I woke up sweating and scared. In the morning I would try to get word about him from my contacts in Sudan, but with the world exploding all around them, it wasn't exactly easy to take the time or find the means to reassure some guy sitting in California that one kid was okay. I did manage to get a few sketchy reports that Daniel had survived the renewed violence, but they did nothing to stop the nightmares.

I managed at one point to Skype with Philippe, the guy who ran the diocese operation in Yida. He was terribly shaken up and told me about one atrocity after another: Women killed in front of him. Men beheaded. Babies shot for no reason. At one point, a man who was fleeing the rebels ran into Philippe's compound to hide, and everyone held their breath, knowing that if he were discovered, they would all be killed along with him.

The connection cut out while I was talking to Philippe, and I was left, staring at my computer screen. I got up and walked around the house, numb and dumb. For days, although I tried to hide it from my family, I was in a kind of post-traumatic-stress haze. I was looking at everything differently—food, water, people's health, all that we take for granted. Just flushing the toilet, or turning on the faucet and watching the water go down the drain, would throw me into a funk. When you've seen people walk for days—days!—just to get a jug of water, the fact that you can turn on the faucet and absentmindedly leave it running and not give it a second thought is completely, thoroughly, utterly, incomprehensible.

A friend once described grief to me this way: Imagine a wheel with just one spoke. Now draw a spiral from the center of that wheel, out to the edge. As you move along that spiral, you pass the single spoke pretty often at first, but less and less often as you move further out along the wheel. That spoke is your grief. Each time you move around the wheel on that spiral, you experience that grief again; it remains intense, but it happens with decreasing frequency.

I first heard that concept right after my father died, and it was a good explanation of how I was feeling. I'd have very intense emotions when I thought about him, but later I would experience waves of guilt because I realized I hadn't been thinking about him for a while. My friend counseled me not to feel guilty—that those waves of emotion were the natural progression of grief.

Now, I was feeling that way about my friends in the Sudan. I would think of them and have intense feelings of grief and sadness for what they were going through; but as the days went by I'd think of them just a little less often, and then experience a wave of guilt for having turned my attention away. As though maybe somehow thinking of them would help protect them—as irrational as that is, we all think and feel that "keeping someone in our prayers" is a tangible, viable way to help them.

And maybe it is.

I felt guilt on all sorts of levels. We had hired a young man in Yida named Alexander to work full-time on Project Daniel after we left. We'd planned to set up a shop for him in Yida, to keep working and printing arms, but when Yida was evacuating, there was nothing left for him. So we'd given him hope, the hope of a job and a goal and a productive life, shown him the promised land, and then it all went up in smoke. It was always my main goal, with Tempt, with the folks in Sudan, with everyone, not to build up any hopes that we couldn't deliver on. And now we had done exactly that with Alexander. So now I'm leaving the house to go get a smoothie at Jamba Juice, and he's got nothing, nothing, nothing.

Damn.

Two things pulled me up from the grand funk that I had fallen into.

One was my boys: You just can't have a long face on when your kids come home from school. You just put on a cheerful expression, and say, Hey, guys, how was your day? And you let their jibber-jabber and their hustle and bustle take your attention, and you allow your love for them to rise up and wash over you, and you ride the wave of it and let it carry you where it carries you. And sometimes, that's enough.

That was a big part of it.

The other was this Not Impossible thing we had created had taken on a life of its own.

Before I left for Sudan, all sorts of projects were bubbling up from the Not Impossible Labs. But there was also a problem with the EyeWriter that had surfaced.

That problem would lead to our next invention.

The EyeWriter had stopped working for Tempt. He simply couldn't fast-blink anymore, and without that, the device wouldn't work. It was a hard blow for all of us.

The Tobii folks, God bless them, had donated a new and better device for Tempt. Like the previous machine, it didn't use the "blink" click that we used—it allowed him to still be able to "speak" through the dwell function. As with the MyTobii, the user lets his gaze linger on a letter for a predetermined amount of time, and the cursor recognizes that as a click.

Given the exposure Tempt's story had gotten, we would probably be able to continue to get him expensive commercial devices that could bypass his problem. But that wasn't the point. Our goal—and Tempt's goal now, too—was "help one, help many." We all wanted to figure out how to make the EyeWriter itself work—not just for Tempt, but for hundreds or maybe thousands of others who would need it.

So we tried readjusting and recalibrating the EyeWriter, but it just wouldn't work anymore. And if it wasn't for making our story public, and open-sourcing how the EyeWriter was made, the story of the EyeWriter would have ended there.

But it didn't.

◆

In London, Ontario, about two hours outside Toronto, there lived a young man who was working as a software engineer for General Motors. One night this young man was a little bored, and started kicking around the internet, and tripped across a TED Talk by a tall, bald white guy who was going on about something called the EyeWriter, and some graffiti artist, and how the EyeWriter had let the artist paint again. And in the TED Talk, the tall, bald white guy was saying something about "If not now, when? If not me, who?"

And something in that thought resonated deeply in the soul of that young software engineer.

And so began the Not Impossible journey of Javed Gangjee.

Javed sent us an email in July 2011, right after he saw my TED Talk, telling us that he had a BA in electrical engineering and asking if there were anything he could do. We wrote him back and told him that we were putting together a team of volunteers to figure out how we might help Tempt move forward.

You never know how these things are going to affect people; they might be very emotional at first, but as the days wear on and the feeling passes, the desire to help might recede. Or, as with me at first, it might take a while before you actually motivate yourself to take some action. But Javed was motivated right away. And he decided to take the first step that he needed, in order to help Tempt: he went back to school.

When you try to figure out how to get people to spend enormous amounts of their time and psychic energy on a project, any project, you have to first figure out what will motivate them. In the workplace, money is usually the motivating factor; but it's not the only one, and not even always the best one. The beauty of the Not Impossible concept is that we don't actually have to motivate people—we just put the problem out there and wait for motivated people to find us. In Javed's case, he was kind of bored at work, and yet the kind of work he was doing was his passion, his calling; it was what he wanted to do for the rest of his life. That was his motivation: he needed to find a way to make that calling more meaningful for himself. The EyeWriter project provided him with that.

At the same time Javed was going to school to learn more of the mechanical skills he needed to go with his engineering skills, he used the EyeWriter as a project in all of his courses, so he had the school's labs at his disposal—and, by default, at our disposal. For example, he needed to take a course on imaging. So he structured his course project around creating a new, better EyeWriter.

Within a month, Javed had built his own EyeWriter. And immediately, he realized it could be improved upon. The first thing he did was to make it simpler. He decided it had to pass what I call the "mom test"—that anyone's mom should be able to build one—but he took it to an extreme. He tried building it mostly out of stuff you'd find around the house—so he challenged himself to use a coat hanger for a mount.

And son of a bitch—it worked.

Then he simplified our lighting system. He decided the four infrared lights we used to illuminate the eye were unnecessary—he thought that simple sunlight could do the trick. So he turned off the infrared lights and turned his device toward the window.

And son of a bitch—it worked.

This kept going—he stole a regular old incandescent lightbulb from a hallway at school and figured out how to make that work for his device. So before you knew it, he had an EyeWriter that you could build for fourteen rather than seventy dollars.

That still didn't do anything for Tempt, of course, but it was the start—and more important, it was a seed, because some of his classmates got wind of what he was doing and got interested as well. So suddenly, we had a little think tank going on.

And here's what they thought of next.

The dwell function that Tempt was using to communicate just wouldn't work with the EyeWriter's drawing program. Javed adapted another open-source program for Tempt's use; but unfortunately, the problems didn't stop there. It was the dwell function itself that had become the problem.

The dwell function can carry with it what's known, in the ocular-tracking community, as the "Midas Touch Problem"—just as

Midas was cursed by the fact that everything he touched turned to gold, so was Tempt cursed—sometimes, he would be just looking at something, and the computer thought he was clicking on it. Midas needed to be able to turn his power off and on—turn lead into gold, but not his wife—just as Tempt needed to be able to turn the cursor on and off. The dwell concept was just too crude, too inaccurate, too unnatural to be really useful. And even though Tempt had gotten really good at it, it was frustratingly slow.

And his eye muscles were continuing to get weaker. No one knew how long he would even be able to use the dwell function.

The answer, if there was one—and you know by now that I believe there always is one—had to lie somewhere beyond his eyes.

And Javed hit on the answer: Tempt's brain.

His brain, Javed reasoned, was still functioning. Why couldn't we use that?

And so, in that moment, Javed turned an idea into gold.

◆

I talked to Javed after that think-tank session, and he asked if we could front him the money to buy an Emotiv. This was a device that Javed had seen in another TED Talk—a commercial device that registered brain waves, a kind of low-cost EEG headset.

As a test, they hooked up the Emotiv to the EyeWriter, with some zip ties, some plastic, and a piece of wood.

And son of a bitch, it worked.

Things moved quickly after that. We started calling this Frankenstein of a device the BrainWriter and started improving on it immediately. We started saying that our goal was to go from "blink" to "think." And we were getting there.

Javed dropped by a local cancer research lab that had a 3-D printer and explained to them what he was doing, and they lent him the printer for the project. So now he and some friends who were helping him out were able to design and create, in a matter of days,

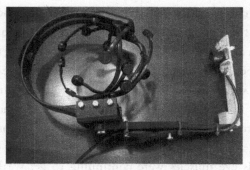

Javed's jerry-rigged Emotiv.

a proper mount for attaching the Emotiv to the EyeWriter. A simple electrical connection meant that you could use your eye to move the cursor, and your brain to say "click."

But how do you get your brain to say "click" in a way that the Emotiv would understand?

Well, you don't, exactly. Here's what you do.

Everyone has all sorts of electrical activity buzzing around near the surface of the scalp. The EEG picks up that light electrical activity. At first, it's just like a radio, picking up random static. But when you think really hard, your brain emits a little surge of electrical impulse—and if you think of something specific, that surge can have a specific signature. The trick is to find a signature that you can identify. For example: Clench your teeth hard, right now. The brain activity that goes along with that effort has a specific signature. Slap your hands together—different action, different electrical signature. Now we have two things that can be identified by the EEG—and we can assign one of those the function of "click the mouse." Even if you can't clench your teeth—just as Tempt couldn't—the mere act of trying to clench your teeth, unsuccessfully, generates a specific brain pattern, which the EEG could identify. The trick is to find something in the user that generates that specific, repeatable pattern. It might be thinking of the word *banana* or *kangaroo*. Find the right thought, and you can click the mouse.

Which is all very good, in theory. But what works in the lab doesn't always work in the real world. So now it was time to take Javed's theory, his EyeWriter, his Emotiv, his coat hangers, and duct tape, and all the rest, out into the world.

It was time for Javed to meet Tempt.

◆

Javed was kind of nervous when he walked into Tempt's room, just as I had been. But even in his paralyzed state, Tempt has such a presence about him, such a sense of grace, that he transmits a feeling of relaxation and confidence to his visitors. Through his Tobii device, Tempt gave Javed a simple "Hey dude, how's it going?" His calm, casual air—and what Javed called "the inexplicable energy of his presence"—made Javed relax, and he got right down to work.

Javed started by setting up the EyeWriter that he'd built—and nothing happened. You could tell Javed was sweating bullets, but there was nothing to do but give him time to get the thing working.

But he couldn't.

Tempt couldn't speak at all because we'd moved his eye tracker slightly off to the side to give Javed room to work, but you could see him smiling inside and you could almost hear him thinking, Hey, hotshot, having a little trouble there? Amazing how Tempt can give people a hard time without saying a word. Javed locked eyes with him for a second and sensed that Tempt was somehow ragging on him, and he couldn't help but start laughing.

The attendants hooked Tempt's eye tracker back up while Javed worked through the afternoon. Little by little, the two of them started talking, like a couple of old friends catching up after a long absence. It was touching how well Tempt connected with Javed. They yakked about life, and politics, and sports, and at one point, Javed started talking about how he wasn't really happy at his job, and Tempt said,

"I guess they just pay you enough so that you can't leave?"—and that kind of stopped Javed in his tracks. Later, he told me that Tempt had really got him to thinking about why he was staying in his job, and that that conversation had solidified his resolve to continue on his school journey. It was an inspirational moment for Javed.

Tempt has that effect on people.

At one point Tempt asked Javed where he liked to go for burritos, and Javed admitted that he'd never eaten a burrito in his life. Tempt's eyes got as big as Ping-Pong balls, and it suddenly became the most important question in the room: where Javed should go for burritos. Realizing how much Tempt wanted Javed to experience this—to experience something he, himself, could never experience again, ever—gave Javed the chills. It was a moment of such kindness, such selflessness, that Javed felt humbled.

Tempt has that effect on people.

At the end of the day, Javed still couldn't get his EyeWriter working and left pretty frustrated. He came back to my house that night, and I managed to scrape him off the ceiling—someone who has butted up against failure as many times as I have is good at getting other people to accept it as a next step rather than a last step, I guess. Once he calmed down, we meticulously went through what could have gone wrong. By the next day, back in Tempt's room, we'd found our answer. The other, commercial eye tracker was interfering with Javed's device—it had magnets in it, and because we'd left it close to Javed's camera, the magnets were messing with Javed's EyeWriter.

Javed got the EyeWriter half of his contraption working and brought in the other half—the brain-reading Emotiv. Unfortunately, it only caused more headaches. Literally. The thing was so uncomfortable for Tempt that Javed couldn't even get it positioned right, let alone try to get it working. We were all frustrated. Everyone agreed it was time to go back to the drawing board.

But Javed wasn't going back alone.

◆

My friend David Putrino, the world-class brain scientist and physical therapist from Australia, had been working on another Not Impossible project when we'd grabbed him up for Project Daniel. Even before I left for Sudan, he was working with Javed on the BrainWriter.

A few months before I'd met David, he had been out drinking with a friend of his—and it's amazing, really, how many of these stories start with "he was out drinking with a friend of his"—when he heard about this guy in Canada who was working on letting an ALS-paralyzed artist draw through use of an EEG device and an eye tracker.

"Sounds like something right up your alley," the friend said to David. "You should ring him up."

How many times does someone in a bar tell you, Hey, I know someone who does something similar to what you do, you should give him a call? A lot. And how many times do you wind up making that call? Not a lot.

But how much of this whole Not Impossible world keeps spinning because someone happened to make one of those calls? A whole lot.

When David made that first call to Javed, they immediately, in David's words, "nerded out together."

"Working in the scientific field, you kind of run into 'yes' people and 'no' people," David told me later. "There are the scientific people who are the skeptics, who just say there's just no way this can be done. They just throw up a couple of roadblocks in front of you and grumble about it. And there are people like me and Javed who say, this is totally impossible, but we're just gonna try and do it."

When you put two people together who have that mind-set of *Let's just say we're going to do this and figure out a way to do it afterward*, interesting things start to happen. Especially if you add alcohol.

"Let's just say," David added, "that there's a lot of whiskey involved in this story."

Here's what happened: A few weeks after that first conversation between David and Javed, David's brother, Gino, happened to be in town, and Gino happened to be an electrical engineer, so one night, they talked it over. If the Emotiv brain-reading device was too uncomfortable for Tempt to wear, what's already available that looks more comfortable and at the same time is affordable? The answer was, basically, nothing. So they did another shot and said, Heck, we'll build one from scratch.

A few cheap electrodes and some conductive cloth later, they had the basis of an EEG—but needed to find a way to press the electrodes against the skull. And in the wee hours of the morning, they decided to use . . . an old sock.

As David said, there was a lot of whiskey involved in this story.

They pressed forward, Velcroing the electrodes into the sock, hooking it up to what's called a "breadboard"—a simple electrical circuit sorter—downloading a free audio recording program, and plugging the makeshift EEG into the audio jack of the computer, where you'd normally plug in a microphone. The whole thing looked like your kid's ninth-grade science project.

They wrapped the sock around David's head and checked to see if they were getting any sort of a signal.

And son of a bitch—it worked.

There were a lot of bugs to work out, of course—getting the electrodes to ignore the background noise was tricky—but sitting in a quiet room, wearing the electronic sock on his head (and *there's* a phrase I bet no one ever wrote before), David did a simple test.

He blinked.

And Gino looked at the monitor they'd hooked up, and sure enough—when David blinked, there was a noticeable, repeatable, recognizable surge in his brain activity.

You can't really imagine the thrill of making something like this work—think of it, a working EEG built from scratch in the middle of the night by a couple of guys who've never tried anything like this before. And I can't underestimate how thoroughly impossible this task was: a journalist we know who covers this field doesn't want to write about the BrainWriter because people have been trying to integrate EEGs into all sorts of devices, and it's a field, he said, "that is littered with dead bodies." And yet, here they were, sitting in the kitchen with a bunch of wires and electrodes, sitting at the threshold of a dream.

"It was a bit of a mad scientist moment—it's alive!—and once again the whiskey comes into play here," David said. "It probably added to the excitement of the situation. But we were very, very happy that it was working."

Now, getting something like this working in your kitchen at three in the morning and producing a device that will actually work for people in the world are two very different things. There was still the problem of background noise, which is not really sound—the electrodes are not really microphones, but they are picking up electrical signals, and in any environment all sorts of things are giving off subaudible electronic signals. Anything you plug in gives off a kind of hum at about 60 hertz, for example. You don't hear it, but it's there.

There's also the problem of movement. EEG devices often don't work because any slight movement creates friction that gives off signals to the system that interfere with the process. In this case, though, Tempt's affliction turned out to be a great advantage, because there are a lot of things he can't do, but one thing he can do—that he can't help but doing—is lie perfectly still.

In the months that followed, while I was away in Sudan, Javed and David kept working on refining their system. They replaced the old sock with an athletic headband, for starters. And replaced the homemade sensors David had fashioned out of foam and conductive cloth with conventional commercial ones. And made a great open-source circuit board to replace their makeshift breadboard.

As of this writing, we still haven't tested the new system on Tempt—but that should be coming soon.

Throughout the process, David and Javed found themselves being asked the same question that I was always being asked:

Why in the hell are you doing this?

"Um, it gets me out of bed in the morning?" Javed said later. "I don't know what else to answer. You know, there's a guy named Don, down the street from my in-laws' place, who has ALS, and he isn't able to get an eye tracker from the government because here in Canada we've got the full health care, so there's a long wait to get your eye tracker, but we don't even know if he's even gonna live that long. So I'm creating a custom application for him. And his wife and he are celebrating their twenty-fifth anniversary together, and it's just wonderful to see them together and the love they have for each other. And they told me they wanted to renew their vows, but he has no way to write his vows. And you think about it, I'm the only one here who can help him. How do you say no to that?"

How do you say no to that, indeed.

Javed wound up hacking together a simple eye-tracker based on a commercial model, and worked up some software in conjunction with a great organization called Speak Your Mind, a fabulous group that works with people who have communication difficulties. The result of Javed's efforts: An eye-tracking communication device that costs under a hundred bucks.

When he tried it out on Don, some of the first words Don spoke—through the machine—were to his wife. "I love you, Lorraine" were the first words she heard. Javed looked over at Lorraine, and saw her beaming with joy.

Now, Javed has caught the fever. "I want every single person who needs this device to get it for less than $100," he said. "And I think we're on our way to getting there. It's a true case of 'help one, help many.'" Sounds awfully familiar.

The difference between makers and the businessmen who came

before them lies not only in the technology available, but in the spirit that moves them. Yes, there are things we can do now with the 3-D printers within the open-source community that were inconceivable just ten years ago. But there's something beyond that: If you tried to create a business based on what these guys were doing, it would be inconceivable. The amount of start-up costs, of research and development and lawyers and office rent and hardware, compared to the tiny profit margins from creating a device that's relevant to such a small portion of the population, would put all of this out of reach.

"So maybe the answer lies within us," Javed told me, "within our own homes, hidden among the coat hangers. Maybe we need to help ourselves, instead of looking to governments, looking to insurance companies. This way, the technology doesn't get held back. The creativity isn't held back by what a lawyer would say or an insurance company would say. The creativity itself has no limits to it."

I guess there's a certain Robin Hood aspect to this—not that we're robbing from the rich, although I guess we're taking some business away from big corporations, though not to a degree anyone's gonna get in an uproar about it—but certainly in that we're giving to the poor. To those who need and don't have. But don't for a second confuse that with altruism—as I said earlier, you have to think of this as a perfectly selfish activity. That's what makes it work—in Javed's words, that's what gets you out of bed in the morning. Not what you're giving out, but what you're getting back.

Take David. As director of telemedicine and virtual rehabilitation at the Burke Rehabilitation and Research Center in White Plains, New York, he takes technologies that won't work with everyone but will work for a certain population, finds those populations, and makes them work. So the fact that he happened to be out having a drink one night with a childhood friend of a guy who was doing exactly that, for Tempt and for Not Impossible—the butterfly effect of that moment is mind-boggling. But you have to come back to the question, What's in it for David?

"A lot of people feel that in this world of tele-rehab, telemedicine, people are afraid that technology will make medicine less personal. So that patients never get to see a real person, they just interact with a computer. What's really important to me about working for Not Impossible is that I get to work on these projects that show the world that technology is making things better, technology is making people have more function, receive a higher standard of care, get to do things that they would never have been able to do even two years ago. And that's really important to me and to establishing that what I'm doing is important. These projects give me street cred. Mick's got this giant mouth, and he's telling the world what I do, and why what I do matters."

Guilty as charged.

◆

The reason it's important to remember the selfish motivation behind the Maker movement is that that motivation—finding a way to do good that's worthwhile to you as well—is essential to the movement's success. It doesn't have to be the rush I get from figuring out how to make arms for a kid in Sudan, or the self-affirming get-out-of-bed rush that Javed gets from working on the BrainWriter, or the what-I-do-matters rush that David says he feels when we broadcast his good works to the world.

It can be as simple a motivation as money. Ain't nothing wrong with that.

The Maker movement comes about because at a certain point, the peasants will rebel. At a certain point, you say to yourself, it's cheaper, faster, or more fun to do it myself than to have someone else make it for me. That might not be the case for cars or large things—although, in the next chapter, I'll talk about some folks who think that is exactly the case for cars and large things—but certainly, on the level we're working at, it makes sense.

But can it make dollars?

Yes. It's been proven to, again and again. Find a niche market, one that will never or could never be served by a big corporation— the profit margin is going to be too small, the cost of start-up is going to be too great. Use the BrainWriter as an example. Once we get it working right, will somebody take our design for it down off the internet, make it better, and start selling it to people who need it? God, I hope so. All you need is to have two links on your site. Here, you want to make it yourself? The code and all the instructions are open source. You want us to make it for you? Happy to. We'll charge you for our effort and time, but it'll still be way cheaper than anything else out there. Consumer's choice; maker's profit. Everyone's happy.

Can you get rich off of that? Not for something with that small a market.

But can you think of another niche that isn't being served, that maybe has a slightly larger market, that you can create a company around, right at home with your laptop and your 3-D printer?

Bet you can.

Many already have.

The revolution is already under way.

CHAPTER 15

The Revolution Against
the Absurd: Your Turn

In January of 2014, Evgeny Morozov wrote a comprehensive history of the Maker movement in *The New Yorker,* tracing its roots back to the Arts and Crafts practitioners of the early 1900s who thought making things by hand would free the souls of the worker who was stuck in the factory. That didn't quite take, but the seed they planted remained—the "celebration of simplicity," Morozov called it, "its back-to-the-land sloganeering, and, especially, its endorsement of savvy consumerism as a form of political activism." That aspiration resurfaced, he points out, with Stewart Brand's publishing of the *Whole Earth Catalog* in 1968, which was geared to people who were dropping out of the mainstream.

What some people forget about Brand is that, as much as he was plugging natural soaps, woodstoves, and tools for drilling your own well, he was also celebrating a nascent technology—the personal computer—as the ultimate tool of emancipation. It was Brand who popularized the term "hackers." As Morozov writes:

> In 1972, he published "Spacewar," a long and much read article in *Rolling Stone* about Stanford's Artificial Intelligence Laboratory. He distinguished the hackers from the planners, those rigid and unimaginative technocrats, noting that "when computers become available to everybody, the hackers take over." For Brand,

hackers were "a mobile new-found elite." He seemed to have had a transcendental experience in that lab: "Those magnificent men with their flying machines, scouting a leading edge of technology which has an odd softness to it; outlaw country, where rules are not decree or routine so much as the starker demands of what's possible." Computers were the new drugs—without any of the side effects.

The students getting beat up by cops were not the real radicals, Morozov quotes Brand as saying. The real radicals were "the holy disorder of hackerdom. A hacker takes nothing as given, everything as worth creatively fiddling with, and the variety which proceeds from that enricheth the adaptivity, resilience, and delight of us all."

When Brand was recently asked who carries the flag of the counterculture today, he responded that it was the Maker movement— the people who "take whatever we're not supposed to take the back off of, rip the back off, and get our fingers in there and mess around. That's the old impulse of basically defying authority and of doing it your way."

Sounds familiar.

In *Makers,* Chris Anderson gives the rallying cry to the whole crazy bunch of us and what we're trying to do: "The past ten years have been about discovering new ways to create, invent, and work together on the Web," he writes. "The next ten years will be about applying those lessons to the real world."

The analogy is perfect: the leap forward in computing and widespread adoption of the internet across the world over the last decade has led to astounding advances in communication, in creativity, in interconnectedness. The people I work with are scattered all over the globe; we share ideas and blueprints and drafts of articles and a hundred other things that would have been impossible, utterly impossible, in my dad's day.

But our ability to take advantage of that kind of interconnectedness, and the limitless creativity that comes from it, have been held back, I think, by two things.

One is the inherent greediness we grew up with. The internet was born of the idea that information wants to be free; people started writing things and throwing them out there, and people started sharing them. A writer would watch his or her words go viral and inspire others and change and morph into other ideas, all at the speed of computers, which doubled every year. Entire governments fell, entire revolutions took shape, because of the freedom of information.

But when it comes to the stuff we create—not the ideas, but the stuff—we've been, as a society, much less willing to give ourselves up to the notion that those ideas—the ideas behind the stuff we create—should also be free. Hard enough to give up on the idea of copyrighting your words—but to give up on the idea of patenting your creation? Horrors!

But that's just what's happening all over the maker world. Just as we made the EyeWriter open source and it got so much better, there are hundreds—thousands—of inventions that have become open source. And then become better.

The other thing that had been holding us back, which we are now liberated from, was the prison known as "economy of scale." Anderson, in his book, uses the example of the Rubber Duckie. Suppose you wanted to go into the Rubber Duckie business. It would cost you $10,000 to gear up—to design the duckie and tool the machine that would churn them out. So it takes $10,000 to get that first duckie made—but after that, just pennies to keep the machine running. So after you've made 10,000 duckies, the cost per unit becomes relatively small.

Still, that's a lot of duckies. If you don't think you can sell 10,000 of them, you probably shouldn't bother. Which means that even before you start, you have to hire people to go do the market research to figure out if it's even worth it—increasing the up-front cost, and increasing the number of duckies you're gonna have to sell.

But in the Maker model, that all goes away. You can design your rubber duckie right on your desktop—and there's no step two in getting it manufactured. If you have a 3-D printer on your desktop as well, that's all you need; the program you drew your duckie with is the same program that tells the printer what to do. You design your duckie; you hit Print; you go have dinner; and, when you come back, there's your little duck. That's it. You can go out and sell it for a couple of bucks, and if anyone buys it, you can make a couple more. No up-front cost of machinery (outside of the printer and the plastic, the costs of which are plummeting every month). No marketing research, no need for the economy of scale.

We are liberated from the need to make only things that lots of people need. Freed to make things that have a limited audience, but an intense one. I don't know how many people will eventually be served by our EyeWriter and its descendants—but unlike every manufacturer of the twentieth century, I don't need to know.

Now, that's revolutionary.

◆

And that's really what we're trying to do with Not Impossible. I would like to see people have greater access to medical devices, communication devices, and other things they need. We makers have disrupted the marketplace and, because we have disrupted the marketplace, people who needed those things in the past suddenly have more access to them.

We started thinking about what we were doing as the Revolution Against the Absurd. Anyone who has tried to get a medical device for a loved one and had to negotiate the maze that's created by the provider, the hospital, the lawyers, and the insurance companies knows just how absurd it can be. It's absurd that in this day and age, an ALS patient would have to communicate with his parents by watching them run their fingers over a piece of paper. It's like seeing someone rubbing two sticks together, and thinking, Hey, someone should invent a match for these people.

In the end, it's about recognizing that it's absurd that certain things don't exist. And that's where all of our ideas came from, and where they are all headed: the simple logic of what should be. We just see the absurdity of these situations and create simple, inexpensive devices that ought to exist in the first place.

Now, the question is, What's to stop some big corporation from just stealing our ideas and running off with them? In the end, we may protect some. We'll see. But the beauty of the system is this: In general, with most of the things we're making there's not a huge marketplace for it. We're not talking about cell phones, where everybody suddenly has to have one. We're talking about what's known as "niche verticals"—small, passionate segments of the population that would otherwise go unnoticed.

And if one of our ideas does catch fire, if we create a device that becomes so popular that large companies want to manufacture it—well, that's a perfect situation as well. That means we've really disrupted the marketplace and found a way to get the big companies to solve a real problem, out in the real world, that otherwise would never have been solved.

And how cool is that.

What we're doing is participating in a radically different kind of reality. In this I feel like we're the children of Buckminster Fuller: "You never change things by fighting the existing reality," he said. "To change something, build a new model that makes the existing model obsolete." I truly believe that's what the Maker model is creating, and what Not Impossible, in our own small way, is touching on: If you start from scratch and build your own reality—even if you're building it out of cheap sunglasses and coat hangers—you can create something beautiful, and lasting, and important. And quite different from the reality that came before.

There is something that happens when you stumble upon a new reality like this. You start seeing it everywhere. I'm sure this was going on somewhere before I got into it—I know it was, in fact—but I was oblivious to it. But now that I've gotten involved, I'm seeing it everywhere—people coming up with ideas to solve problems that would never have been solved before. Solving them at a fraction—a tiny fraction—of what it would have cost had they left it to a big corporation to develop, test, brand, market test, redevelop, package, and produce. The Revolution Against the Absurd is everywhere.

Some of these ideas are germinating at Not Impossible. We are in the early stages of working on a "stutter metronome," a device that helps people talk without a stutter. And a program that would allow parents to tell, early on, if their child is suffering from a very specific form of retinal cancer. And all sorts of other great ideas are starting to take shape.

But we've also made a point, on our Not Impossible website, of trying to get the word out about some miraculous inventions that others are working on, because the sheer size, scope, and genius of the movement is so heartening, so delightful, so mind-boggling, that just to hear about some of the ideas that have already been brought into being gets me psyched and pumped and ready to try the next thing. This newest iteration of the Not Impossible movement is called Not Impossible Now, and I want to share a couple of the stories with you—because I want you to get just as psyched and pumped and ready to try the next thing as I am.

The Do-It-Yourself Wheelchair

Shea Ako is an engineer from Chicago with a very special two-and-a-half-year-old son, Alejandro, who suffers from spinal muscular atrophy (SMA), a congenital neuromuscular disorder, which prevents motor messages sent from the brain from being received by the muscles. He's basically immobile; he has the most severe form of the disease and can moves his eyes, fingers, and toes only a little bit.

"He was diagnosed at the age of about five and a half months," his father told us. "At that time, we had never heard of SMA, and of course we researched it, and we were devastated. All of our visions for the life of our son had to be completely changed."

This is what happens to parents of children with severe disorders. Their dreams change, yet they still have dreams. One mom we talked to told us that, before her daughter's illness, whenever she went to the gas station and saw young people pumping gas, she would think, Please, God, don't let my daughter wind up in a job like that. Today, her daughter is struggling with an as-yet-undiagnosed disorder that has sapped her of all energy and left her in debilitating pain. Now when the mom goes to the gas station, she sees kids pumping gas and thinks, Please, God, let my daughter one day have the strength to do this job.

For Shea and his wife, the dream became that one day Alejandro would have a power wheelchair that he can operate on his own. This is where the absurd part comes in: his family couldn't afford to buy one, and the insurance company refused to pay for it.

"They told us we would have to wait five years because they had already purchased a medical rehab stroller for him" when he was less than a year old, Shea said.

But as difficult as their financial situation was, the technical problem was even more challenging—how could Alejandro, with his limited ability to move, even operate a chair if they obtained one?

Fortunately, Shea has a techie background; he'd worked as a computer programmer and engineer for many years.

So he did what any dad would do. He put everything into making his dream for his son come true.

Shea realized that because Alejandro could apply a little bit of pressure with his toes, he needed to figure out how to let his son use them to guide the wheelchair. Most power wheelchairs operate with some sort of joystick that moves the chair forward and turns it, as well. If Alejandro could only move his toes up and down, how could he turn the wheelchair?

"I thought about how a tank or bulldozer works, where basically you have two controls, and one control controls one tread and one control controls the other tread," Shea said. That was the first germ of an idea. Then, fortunately, the kitchen scale broke. And that was the second.

Shea, being a do-it-yourself kind of guy, took the scale apart to try to fix it. He'd never thought about how a digital scale works before, but when he took it apart he found the magic button inside—the "load cell," which is the basis of operation for that type of scale. He thought maybe he could use something like it as a sensor.

A few cheap digital postal scales and two children's water sandals later, Shea had formed the basis of a chair for Alejandro. He attached the shoes to the load cells from the scales, to keep Alejandro's feet in the right place. When Alejandro flexed his toes, they activated the load cell and sent a signal to one wheel or the other to move forward.

At first, Alejandro was apprehensive about moving the chair. He'd press his toes down, and move a bit, and then sit for a minute or two. It was hard to know what he was thinking, but a boy is a boy, and a motorized chair is irresistible to any kid, let alone one who has been immobilized all his life —and sure enough, once he got the idea, he zoomed off.

Alejandro's right foot is somewhat stronger than his left, so at first he had a tendency to drive in circles. Shea thought about increasing the sensitivity of the left pedal to compensate for that, but Alexandro's physical therapist talked him out of it. Like any kid, Alejandro was facing a challenge, and like any kid, he was gonna try to figure out his way around it. And he learned to compensate on his own for the difference in strength between his feet and balance things out. And move straight forward.

"I think we kind of take it for granted that we can move through space of our own volition," Shea said. "But imagine for a kid who's never been able to change his perspective in the world independently, it's been super great for him. He just loves it. Like any kid, he just loves to explore and move around. We went through a period there where he was crashing into walls—intentionally. Because that's what toddlers do."

And so that's the gift that Shea has given his son: the chance to be as goofy as any other toddler.

And how incredibly, immensely, earth-shatteringly cool is that.

And of course, Shea has put his design out there, open source, in the hopes that other dads can give their kids the same gift. And if that's not the perfect example of help one, help many, I can't imagine what is.

For more information: http://www.notimpossiblenow.com/lives/
awesome-dad-shea-ako

The Make-Your-Own Braille Printer

My kids are huge Lego fans. Like any dad, I used to think Legos were something you gave your kid on Christmas Day and wound up putting together by yourself, grumbling and mumbling, three weeks later. But as time went by, the boys started amazing me with their prowess and patience at putting together more and more complicated Lego sets. I've been watching in awe over the last couple of years as a subculture of people has emerged whose sole purpose in life seems to be making everything imaginable out of Legos—from a full-sized Volkswagen to the Statue of Liberty wielding a *Star Wars* light saber, to some sculptures that boggle the mind both in their complexity and their beauty.

But Shubham Banerjee of Santa Clara, California, saw a need that could be filled with Legos that took this art to an entirely new level. A Not Impossible level, to be precise.

He decided to try to make a Braille printer—out of Legos.

For blind people, Braille can be one of the most important windows on the world—an ability to read and communicate in the most meaningful of ways. A lot of people wonder if Braille is still relevant in a world where text can easily be converted to speech, but none of those people is blind.

Imagine if your child were unable to read or write—and how little patience you would have for someone telling you that reading and writing is irrelevant in today's society because so many books are available as audiobooks. It would be ludicrous for a child with sight, and no less ludicrous for a blind child.

That's where Shubham Banerjee stepped in.

"Over two hundred million people in this world are blind or visually impaired, and ninety percent of those people are living in developing countries," Shubham said. "The normal cost for a normal Braille printer is two thousand dollars and onwards. Can't we do something about the cost?"

That anyone would take on this project is admirable enough. That Shubham took it on is all the more impressive. And touching.

Because Shubham is just twelve years old.

"A lot of people have been thinking a lot about making cool stuff," Shubham said. "I've been thinking a lot about this. We can reduce the cost from two thousand dollars to just three hundred fifty with just a simple Lego set."

Shubham picked up a Lego set called Mindstorms. It came with a set of robotics that, in the kit, was supposed to operate a man made out of Legos but which Shubham was able to modify to make the Braille printer, which he called "Braigo." Essentially, he rigged the Lego robot to make little raised dots on a piece of paper and then programmed it to make those dots correspond to the Braille alphabet.

"This is so easy," Shubham explained, "even my little sister can do it."

*For more information: http://www.notimpossiblenow.com/the
-latest/braille-printer-legos*

The Embrace Incubator

For a class project at Stanford University, a group of graduate students were challenged to design something to treat hypothermia in newborn children. The catch: it had to cost less than 1 percent of the price of a state-of-the-art incubator.

The problem is enormous. Premature babies lack the fat layer they need to stay warm. And hypothermia is life-threatening. Twenty million premature babies are born every year. Four million of them do not survive, mainly due to complications related to hypothermia. And so much of this could be prevented if we could just find a way to keep them warm.

A traditional incubator can cost upwards of $20,000 and requires electricity, so there aren't many available in rural areas of developing countries. Parents try their own homemade solutions—tying hot-water bottles to the babies or placing them under light-bulbs—ineffective at best, unsafe at worst.

The Stanford students—Jane Chen, Rahul Panicker, Linus Liang, and Naganand Murty—met in a class called Design for Extreme Affordability. Right from the start, they were guided by basic principles, similar to the Not Impossible and Maker movement principles: understand the end user; start with the root of the problem, rather than being biased by solutions that already exist; and look for the simplest solution. They were also guided by the passion that comes from personal connection: One of the students, on a trip to India, met a mother whose premature baby had just been born; the closest incubator was in a hospital more than four hours away. By the time they got there, the baby had died.

Nothing could be more motivating than that.

It took them a couple of years to hit on their final solution, but it's a beautiful thing. The Embrace incubator looks like a little sleeping bag for a tiny baby, which you can slip the baby into and Velcro closed. In the back there's a pocket that contains what look like a bunch of packets filled with wax. That material is actually something they call "phase change material"—a substance with a melting point of 98.6 degrees Fahrenheit—human body temperature. You melt them in hot water and slip them back into the pocket, and they maintain one constant temperature for four to six hours. After that you just warm them up again and slip them back in.

The students named it The Embrace, and it fulfills all the needs: it's easy to sterilize, it can be used again and again—and it's cheap. The price point is around $25—and all the research shows it's working as well as those $20,000 incubators.

It's another example of how you can structure a business around an invention like this, and still do the most good for those who need it. There's a for-profit company called Embrace Innovation, based in India, that sells the invention to clinics that can afford it; and a nonprofit, Embrace, based in San Francisco, that takes donations, buys the invention from the for-profit company, and donates them around the world. The for-profit gets investors and creates jobs (right now it employs about seventy and is growing rapidly); the nonprofit is expanding as well, and in addition to providing the baby warmers, creates maternal health programs as well. Embrace now has programs in eleven different countries and has reached more than sixty thousand low-birth-weight and premature infants. It's an incredible and inspiring achievement.

But no delivery of an Embrace incubator is more inspiring than their very first one, on April 9, 2011, in Bangalore, India:

"We faced every challenge that could have possibly arisen in the days leading up to product launch, from a component of the product being stuck in customs, to another not being delivered on time, to the wash tags being placed incorrectly," they wrote on their website. "With an amazing team effort, we were ready to deliver our first product on April 9th. Then, on the way to the clinic, we got a flat tire. Everyone in the car simply jumped out, piled into an auto rickshaw, and hand delivered the first unit to Little Flower maternity home. The experience was truly symbolic: no matter what obstacles we face (or how many flat tires we get), we'll find a way to reach our goals."

Amen to that, brothers and sisters. Amen to that.

For more information: http://www.notimpossiblenow.com/tools/
embrace-warmer-saves-babies

Go Baby Go

Dr. Cole Galloway was doing some fascinating work with movement and early child development in his lab in a child care center in Newark, Delaware. He was learning that, when you enable kids to move around and explore their environment, their ability to learn just explodes. Mobility improves the brain's ability to learn. Most disabled children aren't eligible for a power wheelchair until they're five or six; but Dr. Galloway and a colleague were developing robots that allowed children to move around at a much younger age. The cognitive progress they made, compared to a child who was not mobile, was astounding.

There was a problem, however: The robots they were developing cost upwards of $20,000—out of reach for all but a few families.

But one trip to Toys R Us changed all that.

He realized that he could buy one of those little electric toy cars—the Mater Mobile, based on the character from the movie *Cars*, was one of the first he played around with—and, by adding some PVC pipe and nuts and bolts from the hardware store, could adapt them so that disabled children could ride them.

And Go Baby Go was born.

In his lab at the child care center, Dr. Galloway saw disabled children every day. And the looks on the faces of kids who couldn't walk, who were always left behind by their friends, and who now suddenly were zooming ahead on their motorized carts, was all the motivation he needed.

Dr. Galloway realized that, besides the mobility his device offered to disabled kids, there was a great physical therapy aspect: A little girl named Sara, who had a brain injury and whom everybody thought couldn't hold her head up, got on the device—and soon was holding her head up to see where she was going. A little boy named Xander needed to walk on crutches, but when Dr. Galloway retrofitted his car so that Xander couldn't ride it sitting down, he began standing up—and hopefully he'll soon develop the leg strength to throw away his crutches.

Dr. Galloway made more and more of these devices, until a well-meaning colleague told him he had to slow down and let the patent process work its course, or he'd risk having his invention stolen from him.

"I grew a lot of courage that day," Dr. Galloway said, "and I told him, 'the road to hell is paved with that kind of mentality.'"

That day, he decided to give his invention away.

Flash forward three years: As soon as he open-sourced the Go Baby Go car, people all across the country—all across the world—started building them. He posted videos explaining how to make them and volunteers started Go Baby Go centers from Cincinnati to Poland to New Zealand. He's made more than one hundred of the cars himself—but knows that countless others have been made by folks who have seen his video and decided to become part of his Go Baby Go army.

"We don't run this anymore," he said. "We follow. We just got National Institutes of Health funding to look at this in a very formal way. But we got that funding because of a grassroots effort—families from around the planet. This is a crazy, crazy story. We're a traditional research lab that has been taken over by a grassroots effort of strangers."

Again, that's the beauty of the open-source world. Who knows how many thousands of kids would have grown up, year after year, waiting for the patent process to work its way through the system, waiting for Dr. Galloway to start a manufacturing business he had no interest in starting? Instead, they're moving through their worlds, on their own. Their bodies are stronger, their minds are stronger, they're happier.

And how cool is that.

*For more information: http://www.notimpossiblenow.com/lives/
go-baby-go*

◆

So that's just a fraction of what's going on out there. People taking the backs off things and saying, Hey, I can do this. By the simple act of saying that, by the simple matter of believing that they can do what seemed impossible, the world has changed, immeasurably and irrevocably, forever.

Back at the ranch, we have some pretty impossible dreams for Not Impossible to accomplish. One of the first came out of a trip I made to Mexico.

In May of 2013, I went down to Mexico to experience the Centro de Rehabilitación Infantil Teletón, or CRIT as it's known—the Teletón Children's Rehabilitation Center. The Teletón itself is an annual twenty-four-hour TV and radio telethon that raises money for these rehabilitation centers. My friend, Jaime Camil, a Mexican-born singer and actor who splits his time between Mexico and LA, made the connection for me. I met the founder, Fernando Landeros, and toured the facility in Mexico City. I guess they'd told people I was coming and something about Not Impossible, because one of the young patients had done a painting that was framed for me. It was a painting of him scuba diving in a wheelchair, and if any single image ever captured the spirit of Not Impossible for me, this was it:

That painting sits on my desk to this day.

There are twenty-one of these facilities around Mexico, and each of them is huge. By noon of the day I got there, they had already dealt with twelve hundred kids.

Every step of that tour put me more and more in awe of Fernando and all the people who were running this operation, and all the good that they were doing. But the last stop on our tour, late that afternoon, stopped me in my tracks.

Because I saw something that—quite literally—took kids who were stopped in *their* tracks, and taught them to walk again.

It was a machine known as a robotic gait assistive device—I call it the "Robot Walker." It's a rehab machine for kids with cerebral palsy and other neurodegenerative diseases. It looks like two metal legs, with twelve-inch white elliptical platters where the knee and ankle joints go, with metal rods connecting them together. The child is strapped into what is essentially a weight-lifting belt hung from a simple overhead support grid. The child's legs are placed into the device, and then the child goes for a "walk" on a treadmill. The Robot Walker does all the walking, of course—these children cannot walk on their own, or can barely walk—but it teaches the child what it feels like to have the brain sending signals to the leg muscles. Little by little, the neural pathways re-form, and the children learn to walk on their own.

As we watched, a little girl named Rocío—"dew," in Spanish—a girl who could not walk on her own, was strolling away on the device and smiling at us with a joy that melted your heart.

The device was brilliantly simple and logical. And, apparently, enormously effective: I was told that if a child uses conventional therapy—meaning a therapist working with them manually, with walkers or other typical devices—it takes about five years for the child to walk again. But if they use a robotic gait device, then the children will walk in one year.

I thought, Wait.

What?

One year, instead of five? Why wasn't everyone using these?

I went to lunch with Fernando, and at the first opportunity, I asked him about it: Why, if the device is so successful, don't you have more of them?

Too expensive, he said. The things cost half a million dollars apiece.

I thought, Wait.

What?

And in that moment, I did what has become my modus operandi: I committed first and started figuring out how to honor that commitment later.

"That's ridiculous," I told him. "This is some straps, some carabiners, a rack, some metal rods, and a treadmill. If I could make these for you for a fifth of the price, what would you do?"

His response was immediate. "I'd buy twenty."

So as of this writing, we are about to kick off another hacker weekend and sit down with a bunch of guys who are a whole lot smarter than me to come up with a better and cheaper solution for Rocío.

I haven't the slightest idea of how we're going to hack this thing. And I haven't the slightest doubt that we're going to do it.

◆

What I could never have imagined, though, was the kind of response we were going to get to Project Daniel.

We launched the Project Daniel video at CES in Las Vegas on January 6. Suddenly, the Not Impossible inbox was crammed with requests—can you help my sister, my daughter, my husband, my son. My country.

The first one came from a United Nations group, asking if we could integrate Project Daniel with work they were doing in Uganda. Then we heard from individuals in Pakistan and India. And then a nonprofit in Colombia.

But as overwhelming as all of that was, none of it compared to the email that came next.

It came from something called the Tanzania Albinism Society, which, to be perfectly honest when we first saw it, I assumed was some kind of spam, and I was going to get asked to help a Tanzanian prince get a million dollars into the US, half of which would come to me, of course.

And then I read it.

Dear people of Project Daniel,

Great to hear about your Project Daniel, the 3-D printing project for prosthesis for children in Sudan.

Tanzania has one of the largest populations of people with
Albinism in the world, as many as 170,000 according to some

estimates. Albinism is a genetically inherited disorder. Sufferers are affected by an absence of melanin, a pigmentation defect in skin, hair, and eyes. It causes vulnerability to sun exposure and bright light. Many have very poor vision as a consequence.

Due to an absurd myth that associates people with Albinism with magical powers, they are targeted for their body parts such as legs, hands, fingers, heads and genitals. There is a sinister trade of body parts for the use in witchcraft rituals and good luck charms.

Over the last five years the situation has become much, much worse. Despite international outrages and repeated attempts by the Tanzanian government to stop this appalling practice, the slaughtering continues. Body parts of children with Albinism are most often targeted.

My organization the Tanzania Albinism Society is trying to help these people. Unfortunately we have to work with a small budget and could use all the help we can get.

I also have attached some photos of victims of these attacks.

That's why we love to inform if we could start up a project like Project Daniel for these people.

The Tanzania Albinism Society is run by volunteers, mostly by people with Albinism. We have a head office in Dar es Salaam, next to a hospital. If we could set up such a project, we could not only help the people with Albinism, who lost their hands or legs in these brutal attacks, but also other disabled people in our community.

Hoping to hear from you.

The email was signed by a volunteer from the Tanzania Albinism Society. The photos that accompanied the email were shocking and heartbreaking: Albino men and women and children, all missing fingers and arms. Unbelievable. Elliot read the email as well, and for the longest time, we just kind of stared at each other. We didn't quite know what to say.

But there really wasn't much to say—because there wasn't much of a decision to make.

It was kind of like the decision made itself for us, and was waiting for us to catch up.

And just like that, Project Daniel 2.0 was born. We're calling it Not Impossible Global Labs.

It's taken a lot of logistics and organization, but in the coming months, if we can, we're going to launch a Global Labs project in more than a dozen countries. It boggles the mind, to think of it, but soon we could be creating arms, legs, and other 3-D-printed medical devices—as well as setting up some more simple technology, like brick-making machines—in India. In Sierra Leone. In Haiti, Chile, and Nicaragua. And, of course, in Tanzania.

Wow.

Not bad for a guy who used to just make commercials for a living.

When I give talks about all this, people ask me how many lives I think I'll have changed, when all is said and done. It's a funny question, because I know the answer is—just one.

Just mine.

My journey may have affected a lot of people, and I like to think it has helped some of them, but really, the one who has been most affected by all this is me. I can't begin to tell you the joy that I wake up with each day, having this work to do, having this message to pass along. Of all the self-help books I read, way back when, I never imagined that the message would come back around to me in this way.

Through this whole long, strange trip, I've said again and again, that our battle plan is simple: Help one, help many.

But little did I know that the one you have to help first is yourself. Once you decide that you're going to be really, really selfish and give yourself a life that just makes you smile every morning, this whole world opens up to you. This strange new world. This world that I am so lucky to be a part of.

A world that I hope you'll join me in.

As for what the future holds for Not Impossible, it all feels like something Rod Serling used to say at the beginning of *The Twilight Zone*: we're entering into a wondrous land of things and ideas, whose boundaries are that of the imagination.

And those boundaries become more and more limitless, the more imaginations we add to the mix.

Will we get the Robot Walker done? Will we actually set up Global Labs in all those countries? I sure hope so.

I do know one thing: We have a lot better chance of it if you stop by the Not Impossible website and tell us you'll come along for the ride.

Here. I'll make you the same offer I first made Elliot. I'll write it in this box. It's an offer you can't refuse.

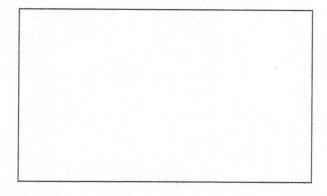

Don't think of it as a blank box.

Think of it as a clean slate. A new start.

Because once you start anew, you never know what comes next.

Because the next thing you know, you just might be doing the impossible.

And how cool is that.

Acknowledgments

Caskey: This is the hardest thing I have written because it deserves the most words. To say you are my rock, my lighthouse, my foundation would be an understatement. You are my reason. It's unfathomable to imagine someone who would know me, support me, and love me as perfectly as you do. You know how to inspire me and ground me all in the same breath. You have given me the three greatest gifts a human could ever imagine—and they look like us! From Isla Vista to today, it seems like a moment but it encapsulates our lifetimes. Thank you for your relentless passion and commitment. Thanks for being my best friend. Thank you for making me and us possible every day, and for twenty-plus years.

Angus, Bo, and Trace: You are the world to me. I wake up every day proud to be your dad. The brave, courageous, kind, adventurous souls that you are make life so much fun. I hope that when you read this book you know that the time I have spent away from you is, by far, the hardest and most impossible thing in my life. Your enthusiasm and curiosity about life are my inspiration and give me hope for the world. If I live a life that inspires you even a fraction of how much you inspire me, then I know it was a life worth living. I love you knuckleheads. You're my knuckle-knuckles.

Mom: It's amazing what happens when I reflect on my life and take a moment to understand why I do what I do; and more important, why I am who I am. It's more amazing when I realize that one

237

of the largest reasons this book could be written is because of who you are, and what you have ingrained in me through your actions over the last forty years. Thank you. I love you.

Lance: If I had a wish for every brother in the world, it would be to have a brother like you. I can't think of a best friend in this world who knows how to push me, challenge me, and make me laugh as much as you do. The memories and life we have shared are at the core of who I am today. I am honored to be called your brother, and look forward to making many more mountain biking, fly fishing, snowboarding, mountain climbing memories together—and soon enough with our own motley crew in tow. Bobo will be smiling down.

Myra: I could not imagine a better partner for my brother or a better sister for me and my family. Thank you for being who you are, in our family and to my brother. Go Bolts!

Enzo: You can't read this yet, but soon enough you will. Just know that you are an Ebeling and by birthright you are expected to go out and adventure, cause a little trouble, and make more than a few mistakes. As your uncle and godfather, I look forward to seeing you grow into your own inquisitive and exploring self and discovering the amazing world that you have the power to change.

Grammy and Pop Pop: You guys are amazing. Thank you for being such an incredible support to our family and to my boys while I am off on Not Impossible adventures. Just knowing that you are with them, loving them, shuttling them, supporting them, and—most important—baking for them brings a smile to my face. Thank you for being so generous and so giving with your time and your love.

Hoot: Thanks for being so good to my mom and for always having so much fun with my boys. Definitely special moments that will always be remembered.

Leslie Meredith: From our very first conversation, you showed that you understand the goal and vision of Not Impossible—the permission to do the impossible. You have been such an incredible support to me on this new journey. Thank you for everything. Just remember our goal around the good book!

Judith Curr: Huge thanks to you, publisher extraordinaire. Your belief in this book, and in what I am doing, is why this book is possible.

And to Donna Loffredo, who has held our hand every step of the way; Paul Olsewski, the world's best (and my favorite) publicist; and to all the team at Simon and Schuster—David Brown, Jackie Jou, LeeAnna Woodcock, Sarah Wright, and incredibly clever and endlessly patient Patricia Romanowski Bashe: Thank you all, enormously. You have taught me what it means to have the best team around you, and I am eternally grateful.

Jeff Kleinman: An unexpected email. That is how this whole thing started. "If you wold be interested in working on a book, would you please let me know? It seems you have a great story to tell, and a book is really a great way to tell it." I never thought about writing a book, and thanks to you, I now have. Thank you for being my Sherpa throughout this new adventure. You have had a relentless passion and enthusiasm around my work from our very first conversation. You always presented logic and options. You constantly helped me prioritize what was in line with the overall goal of the book. You always spoke from a place of reason. And you never accepted anything less than the best. Thank you for your first email. Thank you for making this book possible.

Phil Lerman: Amazing. That is the only word that comes even close to encapsulating the experience I had working with you. From the very beginning, I felt like I was in safe and experienced hands. Your ability to extract the meaningful bits from my memory was nothing short of miraculous. Your ability to seamlessly meld into the Ebeling family and worklife and navigate it so deftly was inspiring. Your ability to own this story as if it were your own just demonstrates your extreme professionalism and talent. But your passion and unwavering commitment to what this book is supposed to be is what makes you a pancake-making, jazz-loving, writing superhero. Thank you for making this book possible, my friend.

Daniel: For as long as I live, I will never forget November 11. On that day, with that bite, you showed the world the meaning of Not Impossible. Your smile. Your spirit. Your perseverance. My boys talk about you regularly as if you are part of the family—because you are. My wish for everyone in this world is to meet a Daniel at some point in their lives. I am truly a better person for meeting you. Thank you.

Tempt: You are an enlightened soul. Someone I look to for inspiration. I will forever be indebted to your generosity of spirit and allowing me into your life. My life is truly better because I met you. You are a role model and hero in our family and we are honored to continue to be part of your life. This adventure started—and continues—because of you. Thank you.

The Quan Family: Who would have thought that this all would stem from that first meeting at The Pantry? That was the start of our journey together and the birth of the concept of Not Impossible. Thank you for allowing Caskey and me into your lives. We were perfect strangers, and your trust in us helped pave the way for everything we now do around Not Impossible.

Dr. Tom: "Preach often. Use words as little as possible." I had never heard that before you said it to me, and it truly is the encapsulation of who you are as a doctor, a Catholic, and a human. Thank you for living that so loudly. Your drive and conviction is something I aspire to. Thank you for your belief and your drive to make the lives of the people of the Nuba Mountains better. Without that drive, we would have never met, and Project Daniel would have never been. Thank you.

People of Mother Mercy and Gidel: Amid a contradiction of a spectacular landscape and horrible injustice, I could not imagine a more welcoming, generous and happy people. I speak with Caskey often about how much I miss you all and ache to return to you. Having been allowed into your lives for a moment has changed my life forever. Thank you.

Richard and Beth Van As: Your generosity was and continues to be simply staggering. Thank you for believing in Project Daniel so much; for traveling halfway around the world, for taking me into your home, training me, preparing me, feeding me, and then sending me off to do what is truly one of the most important and formulative projects I have ever undertaken. Richard, although differences in opinion abound between us (as one would expect from two headstrong SOBs), you will always be the Yoda who made Project Daniel possible. Thank you.

Project Daniel team: DOE. Adrian Belic. Tim Freccia. Peter Mozynski. Phillippe Asseng, the generous people of SP. The passionate people of Mother Mercy hospital. Thank you for being such incredible people and making the impossible project of Project Daniel a reality.

Ollie, Edouard, Beatrice, Lloyd, and the entire Precipart family: Thank you for your passionate commitment to everything Not Impossible. Working with you feels like working with family. You stepped up when the chips were down. You guys came through when Project Daniel needed you most and that is a level of loyalty that I will never forget. Thank you.

Team Intel—Kevin, Donna: What an amazing journey we've been on together. Thanks, Donna, for stepping up and stepping in when we needed you, and to Kevin for being such a huge advocate and ally—you guys were amazing. Thank you.

Venables Bell: Thanks for your incredible support and championing of Not Impossible and Project Daniel. Paul, Tom, Eric, Ezra, Rob, Craig, Kate, Erik, Joe, Kara, Sarah, Jillian, Meredith—you guys were amazing to work with. I always felt like you were fighting for the best creative and thoroughly appreciate your tireless support of Project Daniel.

Will McGinniss: Dude. Thank you. You believed. You took a risk. You delivered. Thanks for leaving it all on the court and going with your gut. I got your back—whenever, wherever.

Tribe: Blackers, Grahams, Moffets, Tuttles, Blairs, Fulfords, Wan-Reeses, Dhurvas. To have family like the Tribe is to have heaven on earth.

Mike, Chris, Robert: A person lives his whole life hoping to have friends like you guys, and I was lucky enough to have had you as a vital part of my life for more than half of my time on this planet. I could write an entire book on the memories and fun we have had together over the years. Thank you for the years of laughter and good times. Thank you for Jawbone. Thank you for Bali. Thank you for the treasure box. Thank you for your kids, whom I love as my own. Most importantly, thank you for your continued love and friendship, even though I am most likely the worst-communicating friend you have. Just know that in the sometimes-significant gaps between speaking to or seeing each other, my love and appreciation for our friendship only grows stronger.

Letter-writing friends and family: To all the people who wrote me those letters while I was in Sudan. Those letters kept me going but more importantly, those letters reminded me how lucky I am to have such incredible people in my life. Thank you.

Tor: Homie. Thanks for being a constant advocate and believer. Having you as a sounding board and supporter gives me such confidence. Having you as a friend is gold. Let's make sure we continue to break some ribs every year and laugh at our own feeble mortality in some quasi-adrenaline-soaked way.

Paul Lavoie: Monsieur. Thank you for everything you do. The advice. The introductions. The meals. The wine. The lodging. All part of the perfect way you support me and believe in what I set out to accomplish. Thank you.

Tom Dunlap: Thanks for always being such a great fan, champion, and friend. Thanks for making sure that we had a plan B when

I was in Sudan and for giving Caskey the confidence and security she needed while I was away.

Will Travis: Thanks for your belief and passion in me and around everything I have been doing. You have always been a fan and supporter. I am inspired by you: Your clarity, your drive, and your relentless commitment to adrenaline. I look forward to the evolving future role you will play in Not Impossible, whatever that may be.

Kyle Brown: Holy cow. What an amazing ride. And I am not just talking about the Fireflies. Thank you for your unquestioning and unflappable belief in what I am up to. You have poured your heart and soul into every single thing we have done together, without even the slightest hesitation. Thank you for your talent, your commitment to what I am trying to accomplish, and your unflappable loyalty. I am beyond lucky to have a friend and editor of your caliber all wrapped up in one great package. Thank you.

Steve Mykolyn: Thanks for always being such an amazing friend, fan, supporter, and hotelier—and art-buying-addiction starter.

Mike and Matthew: Although the relationship is brand new, the strength of your belief in Not Impossible is so apparent. I look forward to seeing how the future unfolds.

Elliot: Maaaaaate. Where to begin . . . You are a quiet force of nature. You are low word count, high results. Your ability to spontaneously generate and strengthen ideas is awe-inspiring. You embody everything we stand for at Not Impossible, and this wouldn't be nearly as much fun without you. Your untiring belief and commitment comes through so loudly in your post-midnight emails. Thank you for the bad puns, the hysterical laughter, the vision, and, of course, for Sam. I thank you.

Megan and Sophia: You two are powerhouses and constantly remind me of how much fun it is to work with passionate, smart, dedicated, fun-loving people. Thank you for your belief and your drive to make Not Impossible reach its fullest potential.

Not Impossible team: Working with you guys has been an honor and a privilege. If I can continue to live my life surrounded by passionate and talented people such as yourselves, then it will be a good life to look back on.

David: Thank you for your relentless belief in Not Impossible. Your willingness to jump on an airplane on five minutes' notice, your strategic thinking, your inability to say no to anything we are doing. This is why we are where we are as an organization. Thanks for your ever-present New York hospitality—and for not letting Rose steal my buckwheat. Rose, you are a giant. But you know that. Thank you for everything.

Javed: Not sure where to begin in expressing my gratitude to you. I could not imagine being more blessed than to have you as the inaugural Not Impossible mad scientist. Your relentless passion and conviction are contagious, and inspire everyone who comes into contact with you. Thank you for being the incredible, brilliant, talented, compassionate human being you are. Thank you for embodying everything that Not Impossible stands for.

Mike, Alex, Alan: Huge, huge thanks for always protecting the fort and keeping things possible. Mike, you have been a great friend and confidant for my entire professional career. I don't see how Not Impossible or TEG could have been possible without you there for us. Alex, your deep caring for me, my company, and my family is something that I appreciate to depths unquantifiable by words. Alan, having you in my corner is what makes it possible to sleep soundly at night. Thanks for being strong, strategic, and yet always human and passionate about what I am up to. Thank you all.

Scott Hidinger: Not sure you formally signed up for being the NI creative director, art director, and brand manager. (Actually, I am sure: you didn't.) But you constantly and consistently show up and make us better. Thanks for being our creative-brand-visual sherpa. Thanks for the incredible book cover. Thanks for being an amazing (and spontaneous) friend who is always willing to jump on an Ebeling adventure just about to leave the station.

Pete, Rick, Vic, Dana, Ted, Cara, and the rest of Team Deutsch: Thanks for the incredible cover design. You guys are amazingly talented and generous. Thanks for bringing the vision of Not Impossible to a visual reality for the cover.

And finally: To the readers of this book. You are the reason we have undertaken this project: so that you can hear what we're about. And, hopefully, so that you will join us. There's so much room at the inn—and so much need for like-minded travelers. See you at the next Maker weekend.

You bring the sleeping bags. I'll make the pasta.

Index

Page numbers in *italics* refer to illustrations.

About the Author

Raised in a family of entrepreneurs and philanthropists, Mick Ebeling is the executive producer and founder of The Ebeling Group, an international production company and creative think tank, and he is the recipient of nearly every advertising award, including the Titanium Cannes Lion. He is also the founder of Not Impossible, an organization that develops accessible, creative solutions to real-world problems. An internationally acclaimed speaker, Ebeling has spoken before Fortune 500 companies and given multiple TED talks on the subject of making the impossible possible. He has received several awards for his humanitarian work, including, most recently, the 2014 Muhammad Ali Humanitarian of the Year Award.

He lives in Venice Beach with his wife, Caskey, and three sons.